FUTURES HANDBOOK FOR FARMERS

By
DEAN NOSKER

SECOND EDITION

DOANE
PUBLISHING

Doane Publishing / 11701 Borman Drive / St. Louis, MO 63146

Second printing — 1984
First printing — 1981

First Edition 1979

ISBN 0-932250-13-0

CONTENTS

Page

INTRODUCTION 5
THE SPECULATOR 7
PRINCIPLE OF "GOING SHORT" 11
"CARRYING CHARGE" MARKETS 14
THE SPECULATOR'S ROLE IN SPREADS 16
MARGIN REQUIREMENTS 19
THE BROKER 23
THE TECHNICAL MARKET 25
CHART PRICE PATTERNS 27
OPEN INTEREST AND VOLUME 36
KNOWING YOUR BASIS 40
THE STORAGE HEDGE 43
HOW BASIS CHARTS HELP 49
BASIS GUIDES HEDGING DECISIONS 54
DELAYED PRICING: NOT FOR THE INEXPERIENCED 57
"BASIS CONTRACT" LESS RISKY 60
USING LIVESTOCK FUTURES 63
LIVESTOCK HEDGING EXAMPLES 65
THE BUYING HEDGE: AN OPTION FOR FEEDERS 67
SAMPLE CONTRACT SPECIFICATIONS 71
GLOSSARY 75

INTRODUCTION

Most commodity traders are city oriented. Many have never been on a farm. The farmer's interest certainly isn't paramount in their thinking. They're in the markets to make money, clear and simple.

These speculators are complemented by the huge, knowledgeable grain merchandisers, packing houses, export houses, and other trade interests. Some may be more sympathetic to the farmers' plight than the speculators. But the farmers' interest certainly isn't paramount in their thinking either. They're in the market to make money, and for protection against unfavorable market developments.

But, what about the farmer? With the tremendous growth in commodity market participation, it's a paradox that farmers have not greatly increased their dealings in the futures markets, even though they make up one segment of the economy the markets were designed to help.

Farmers hesitate to use futures because they don't understand them. It's a good reason to stay away. But, it's a poor argument for not learning more about commodity futures. The cash offers you receive are tied directly to the futures markets.

You can be sure most of the trade people you sell to have a good command of your area basis and know how to use it to advantage in making cash purchases. If you lack that knowledge, you know less about some important aspects of your product than the person you're selling to, normally not an enviable position in any business transaction.

This handbook is mostly about hedging, because that's what the futures markets are about. It's not intended to convince you to use the commodity markets for hedging (although we hope it helps you see merit of storage and production hedges). Nor is it intended to keep you out of the markets.

However, we do believe you need some knowledge of the futures markets, whether you ever intend to hedge or not. Action in futures markets, including chart movement, can be helpful in your cash marketing program also.

We're trying to explain an extremely complicated industry in simple terms. What you read here won't make you an expert; far from it. You'll need further help from someone with daily market experience, such as a reliable broker.

However, we hope these few pages will make you better able to choose a broker, to test his reliability, and to better understand his language. And, we hope to sell you on the value of price charts and the role they can play in your marketing program, whether it be through hedging or strictly cash sales.

The Speculator

You may feel it's a strange assortment of bedfellows, this group that makes up the speculative segment of commodity trading—but it's because of (rather than in spite of) this group that the commodity markets can be of any use to you at all. Speculators can give the market the liquidity necessary for farmers to put hedges on and take them off quickly and efficiently.

The speculator is an integral part of the futures market. If you're going to hedge, you need to know what he's about. You also need to know what he's about if you don't hedge, because at times the speculator is a prime influence in the futures and, therefore, the cash markets.

An awareness of chart formations and how they can benefit your marketing is in reality an understanding of the people who use the futures, both trade and speculative. They are the forces that build and subsequently react to chart patterns.

Who is the average speculator? He is not normally the older, established, well-to-do businessman looking for a new investment in life.

There are some in this category, but generally people in this age bracket have already established their investment patterns and aren't disposed to change them to include commodities.

A veteran commodity trader is judged so, not by his age, but by how long he has been trading. He's a veteran because he has taken his lumps and has learned to handle himself in the markets. He may not be rich for his efforts, but he's cagey. He's won his spurs.

The percentage of these veteran traders in the commodity markets is almost minuscule compared to the whole. At any one time they are vastly outnumbered by novice traders who will give up the battle after the first skirmish.

They come into the markets because they've read it's too dry in the Southwest, or there is corn blight in the Midwest, or TGE is running rampant in the nation's farrowing houses, or for a myriad of other reasons—most of which, if they take the hoped for course, spell impending disaster for the farmer.

Does this make the speculator your enemy—an adversary who wants to do you in? No. You would find the majority of speculators likable and interesting, full of energy, well educated, personable—young men on the way up. If their success depends on your being done in, it's not for personal reasons. And, quite often in their two-fisted, guns blazing, headlong plunge to buy commodities, speculators can help improve your sales opportunities by pushing markets well above economic value.

Impending disasters attract the speculative public because most people coming into the commodity markets for the first time would rather be "bulls" than "bears."

Selling short appears to go against the natural bent of the American psyche. Maybe it's just part of our makeup—an eternal optimism inherited from the nation's pioneers.

That may be part of it. But, it's also easier to visualize Kansas wheat wilting under a relentless sun and pelted by wind-driven dust than to spend tedious hours studying supply-demand prospects and the hundreds of other factors that may indicate bigger than needed supplies and probable price decline—even if you had the experience and necessary facilities to make such a study.

In any event, most speculators would rather be bulls than bears. The most spectacular bull moves occur when both the speculator and the trade are actively involved in the price making.

You lived through numerous examples of this in recent years as grain supply shortages had both speculators and users scrambling to buy.

There are many less dramatic price moves where speculators play the dominant role. Often these moves are based more on anticipation of a potential market force (such as weather damage) than on a real bone-crunching problem that threatens supply and gets the trade involved, too.

During the hectic first days of a speculative move, prices rise quickly. They hit a peak, then back off as some traders, bewildered and overjoyed by their quick profits, sell out their long positions.

Their profit taking causes sharp market price drops which quickly may be erased by a new crop of speculators eager to buy at the lower prices. The up-move, by this time, is a herky-jerky affair.

But, all good things must come to an end. Finally the day comes when there is no longer support on reactions from the highs. It seems that everyone who is going to buy has bought. Lack of concern by the trade takes effect. Some speculators get out with a profit.

Those who joined the bandwagon after most of the move was over now face a dilemma. They have losses. Those who bought at other lower stages of the up-move have a problem too—they may have profits, but they are losing them by the minute. Those who bought at the top scramble to get out. Others follow suit, and the market begins to crumble.

If the panic becomes severe enough, supply-demand fundamentals may not mean much for a time. As was the case on the way up, the speculator is the dominant market force pushing values lower.

Why You Have an Advantage. . .

The majority of speculators (probably more than 90%) lose money. It's a sad fact, but one that should have little bearing on your success.

Here are your advantages as a hedger:

(1) Because the hedger is simultaneously dealing in equal amounts of both cash and futures, he is better protected than the speculator who usually is only on one side of the market. In a price rise, what you may lose in a futures market short position will be compensated for to some extent by increasing value of the actual product which you also own.

(2) As a hedger you are mostly concerned about the long term market trend. The speculator worries about the short term weekly, daily, at times hourly, ups and downs of the market.

Where the hedger may have only one basic decision to make, the average speculator subjects himself to many decisions and can often compound his mistakes with each move he makes.

A temporary supply shortage, a minor drouth scare, a poor export figure, heavier than expected weekly slaughter, a surge of short covering—any of these and more, continually bombard the speculator.

Unless he has extreme confidence in his original plan (if he has one), he may often be right on his long term analysis but still lose money because of in and out trading due to short term day-to-day pressures from the market.

The problem that many farmers have with hedging is that they too fall victim to the short term pressures—and end up not as hedgers but as speculators in their own right burdened with the same increasing number of decisions and just as likely to make the wrong ones under stress.

The successful hedger, as is the case of the successful speculator, has put enough thought and time into the market to come up with a good long-range plan.

Although it's important to keep an eye on market developments, the primary objective should be to follow that plan. If you change it without at least as much thought as you put into the decision to hedge in the first place, you're probably headed for trouble. The minute you begin tampering with your hedge you join the speculative ranks.

Tax treatment of futures transactions gains or losses underscores the difference between speculating and hedging. Gains from hedging are ordinary income, and losses can be deducted as business expenses. There is no limit on the amount of loss that is deductible in a given tax year. Speculation in commodity futures, however, results in capital losses from IRS' point of view.

If you hold a long position for more than six months, any profit will be subject to a special long term capital gains taxation rate. But if a short position results in net gain, or if a commodity contract is held for less than six months, the net amount is fully taxable as short term capital gain.

Principle of "Going Short"

KEY TO THE STORAGE HEDGE

The commodity markets are structured so it's just as simple to go "short" or sell the market as it is to go "long" or buy it.

Many people have trouble with the concept of going short when first exposed to it. Farmers probably don't have as much trouble with the concept as the average speculator, but one of the most common questions beginning traders ask is:

"How can you sell something you don't own in the first place, then turn around and buy it later—at a profit!!"

The speculator goes short the market when he expects the price to drop. If he can offset the sale of a contract through the purchase of another at a lower price, he profits by the difference.

A speculator who sells December corn at $3 on October 1 and then closes out his position by buying an offsetting contract at $2.88 on October 14 has made the 12¢ difference.

Another speculator who went long and subsequently closed out (or sold) a contract on these same days at the same prices would lose 12¢ per bushel (or $600 per 5,000-bushel contract) because he would have to sell at a lower price than he bought.

Here's an on-farm example:

On April 1, you and a neighbor get into a friendly disagreement about what corn prices are going to do in the months ahead. You think prices are headed for a downturn. Your neighbor thinks they will be stronger.

It's an important question because your neighbor has 200 feeder pigs that will take about four months to feed out, and he only has a two-month supply of corn.

The question is: Should he buy the corn now since he expects much higher prices on June 1, or should he wait to buy when he actually needs the grain?

You say he should wait since the price will be lower two months from now. He answers with this proposition: "I'll pay you today's price for 1,000 bushels of corn if you promise to deliver it on June 1."

You accept the deal. You don't own any corn. You will have to buy it at the prevailing price on June 1. You, in effect, are "short" the corn market.

You have sold something you don't own with the hope of buying it later—at a profit!!

If corn currently is selling at $3 per bushel and you are able to buy it at $2.88 on June 1, you have made 12¢ profit per bushel.

In the futures market, the speculative short operates in exactly the same manner, except that he never expects to deal in the physical commodity.

Very few hedgers who have put on a selling hedge (sold futures equal to part of their cash inventory) expect to hand over the actual commodity when the contract expires, either. Trade interests who normally hedge in the futures markets include such businessmen as:

1. Exporters who handle huge quantities of grain in trading operations with other countries.

2. Elevator operators who store quantities of grain bought from farmers.

3. Processors who buy supplies of a commodity to convert it into a salable by-product.

They look to selling hedges primarily to protect their cash inventory if prices drop dramatically while they still own the physical commodity. Here's how they get that protection.

Hedging is based on the principles that:

1. Forces affecting the cash and nearby contracts usually also affect (though normally not to the same degree) the distant contracts representing the same crop year.

2. As each futures contract expires, the cash and the expiring futures contract tend to seek the same price level.

Therefore, if the market goes down, what is lost in the cash product will be offset in part by equal gains in the short futures position.

Even if the cash and futures don't move exactly together, any big drop in cash prices would be reflected to a degree in the nearby futures contract. And what could have been a disaster to the owner becomes much less of a loss because of his short position in the futures market.

"Carrying Charge" Markets

The futures markets are at carrying charges when the distant contracts are selling at higher price levels than the contracts that precede them. Normally, carrying charge markets in grains reflect an ample supply situation.

When the price difference between the nearby contract and successively distant contracts in the same crop year covers the total cost of such hedging costs as storing and insuring, or carrying, the commodity into those months, the market is said to be at "full carrying charges."

For example, let's say at current storage and insurance rates, it costs about 5¢ per bushel per month to store corn.

If December futures were selling at $3 per bushel, a market at full carrying charges would have the March future at $3.15 (3 months times 5¢ per bushel), the May at $3.25, and the July at $3.35.

Trade interests watch the price differences (or basis) between contracts closely. The spread between contracts plays an important role in hedging decisions.

Assume, for example, that in February an elevator manager has corn hedged in May futures. When he placed the hedge in January, the May contract was selling at 8¢ over the March. The July contract was 12¢ over the March.

Therefore, the May was offering 4¢ per bushel carrying charge when the hedge was placed. The July was offering 3¢. May futures were a better hedging opportunity by 1¢ per bushel.

Now it's February. Declining prices have pushed the futures farther toward a full carrying charge. The May is selling at 8¢ over the March. The July has moved out to 18¢ over the March.

At this point, the elevator would see an opportunity to "roll over" his short hedge from the May to the July contract. Why? Because at that instant in time the July is offering better storage earnings—4½¢ per bushel per month in the July versus 4¢ in the May. Here are the prices:

CORN PRICES

Date	Cash	March	May	July
Jan. 10	$3.04	$3.25	$3.33	$3.37
Feb. 10	$2.89	$2.94	$3.02	$3.12
July 1	$2.81	—	—	$2.97

Here are the elevator transactions in rolling over the hedge:

Date	Cash	May Futures
January 10	Bought at $3.04	Sold at $3.33
February 10	$2.89	Bought at $3.02
		–$ .31

The value of the cash corn in storage has dropped 15¢ per bushel. However, the elevator picked up 31¢ profit in the futures transaction which is credited to the hedged corn. He rolls the hedge over into the July contract which is currently 23¢ over the cash. *Based on experience in past years, the elevator expects that basis to narrow in to around 15¢ by July.*

By July, cash corn has moved back to $2.81—a basis of 16¢ under the July futures. The elevator sells the cash and buys in the futures contracts.

Date	Cash	July Futures	Basis
February 10	$2.89	Sold at $3.12	–23¢
July 1	Sold at $2.81	Bought at $2.97	–16¢
		–$ .15	

He picked up another 15¢ per bushel on the July hedge which, added to the $2.81 cash price and the 31¢ picked up in the May hedge, gives a total of $3.27.

He paid $3.04 for the corn. He received $3.27 through the hedging transaction. Had he not hedged, he would have received $2.89 for corn he bought at $3.04.

In any event, you can see why the difference between the nearby and distant futures contracts shouldn't exceed (and often doesn't achieve) the theoretical full carrying charge. Commercial interests who own the grain will automatically keep those spreads in line. *So do speculators.*

The Speculator's Role in Spreads

As already illustrated, a basic working premise behind any hedging operation is that cash and futures prices tend to come together as each futures contract expires.

Also, since the cash and futures contracts in the same crop year are subjected to the same basic economic fundamentals, they should respond alike to those fundamentals—with cash and all same-crop-year futures rising in a bullish situation and all falling under a bearish market influence.

In general, this is the case. However, it should be noted that even though the cash and futures contracts in a commodity may move in the same direction, they seldom move to the same degree over any period of time, and the farther the contract month is from the current cash period, the less the relationship may be.

For example, *in a bull move, the cash and nearby futures contracts will generally rise faster than the distant contracts in the same crop year.*

Conversely, *in a bear market, the cash and nearby futures will normally fall faster than the distant contracts.*

The reason? In a bull market there is a shortage of the commodity relative to demand. High prices are needed to: (1) ration the available supply and (2) stimulate greater production.

In an oversupply situation, the nearby contracts feel the weight of deliveries and the need for values to drop sufficiently to price the surplus into consumption.

No one is interested in storing the product unless there are wide carrying charges in the market because the oversupply has reduced the need for large inventories. This is why the basis between cash and futures normally moves to its widest level and futures contracts spread out toward carrying charge levels at harvest.

Of course, speculators can also play a role in the moves, or spreads, between the cash and nearby and distant futures contracts. Spread traders, knowing that the nearbys may gain on the distants on a bullish development, put on spread positions, buying the nearby contract and selling a more distant contract.

As the market moves up, the nearby contracts should rise more, or at least faster, than the deferred contracts, and the speculator profits by the difference. For example, in an upmove in the corn market a speculator may buy the nearby March contract and sell the July because he expects the March to outpace the July on the way up.

He's attracted to spread trading in the first place because there is less risk than a net position (because, like the hedger, he has offsetting positions in the market). And since there is less risk, spreads require less margin than net positions.

If March corn is selling at $2.81 and July at $2.97 when a speculator puts the spread on, here's how subsequent market action might develop.

On January 10	On February 27	
Buys 1 contract of March Corn at $2.81	Sells 1 Contract of March Corn at $2.96.	Profit 15¢
Sells 1 contract of July Corn at $2.97	Buys 1 Contract of July Corn at $3.05	Loss 8¢
	Net Profit	7¢

In the bullish situation both the March and the July contracts rose. However, the March rose faster than the July. The gain on the "long"side of the trade outdid the losses on the "short" side and the speculator profited by the difference.

You can see how speculative activity of this nature can influence the price difference between the cash and the distant contracts in which a producer may be hedged.

Speculative selling in the July contract helped keep some pressure on its price, while, at the same time, the buying activity in the March also probably would give some support to the cash price which is tied most closely to the nearby contract.

The point is that: (1) while the cash and futures prices generally run in the same general direction throughout the life of a contract, and (2) the cash and futures tend to come together as each contract expires . . . there are influences during the life of each futures contract that can keep it out of complete balance with the cash market.

Situations such as farmer holding, transportation difficulties, out-of-position problems, or other near term bullish developments which strengthen cash prices will generally send them up to a greater degree than the distant futures.

Those gains, of course, will be lost again once the temporary problem is relieved. When supplies are again sufficient for near term needs, the cash price will drop—usually falling faster than the distant contracts.

Why? One reason is those same speculators who aided the bull spread in the first place. When it looks like the problem is solved and prices are headed down again, speculators getting out of the bull spread have to sell out their long nearby position and buy back the short distant position. This, of course, tends to put pressure on the cash and create support under the distant contracts.

There are generally scores of such moves (up and down) among futures contracts during the crop year. However, as the time approaches for a futures contract to expire, you would expect the degree of such fluctuations between that contract and the cash to lessen.

That's because with all the ups and downs and widening and narrowing of spreads between any futures contract and the market your cash offer is tied to, they are inevitably headed on a collision course at the futures delivery point.

Nothing is ever certain in the futures markets, but in general, the less the time period before that collision must occur, the closer you may expect cash and futures to be to each other.

The cash to distant futures relationship (or basis) is generally widest at harvest, then tends to narrow in as time approaches for those futures to expire.

That's the rationale behind the storage hedge—a form of futures transaction that too many farmers neglect.

Margin Requirements

Margin is money that anyone who trades in futures markets, including hedgers, must deposit when they initiate a long or short position.

This deposit is earnest money only, and when you close out a profitable position, the margin required for the trade stays in your account. The only futures expense is the commission.

However, if the market goes against your trade, you may be subject to a margin call requesting additional capital in your account.

If that requirement isn't met within a day or two, your broker has no alternative under exchange rules but to close out your position.

The various exchanges set minimum margin requirements. The minimums generally run around 10% of contract value. Therefore, margin requirements are subject to change if prices rise or fall sharply. When changed, the new margins apply to both new and existing positions. Individual commission brokerage houses can put their margin requirements above the minimum exchange levels, but they can't drop below those levels. Margin requirements and contract specifications for most major commodities are shown on pages 71 through 73.

Speculative accounts work at two margin levels—the initial margin and a maintenance margin. If the Board of Trade initial margin is $2,250 for a contract of soybeans and the maintenance is $1,500, the speculator who wants to buy or sell a 5,000-bushel contract of beans must deposit at least $2,250 margin when the trade is executed.

If he bought at $7.50 and the price goes to $7.80, where he gets out, he has made 30¢ or $1,500 on the trade (30¢ x 5,000 bushels) minus commission (we'll use $60) or a total of $1,440.

His account now is worth $3,690. If he wants to trade another contract of beans, $2,250 of that will be required for initial margin.Let's say he does, and takes the $1,440 profit out of the account for other purposes.

He buys the bean contract at $7.95. But this time prices fall. They reach

$7.62 on the close. His account is now $900 under the $1,500 maintenance level. (The arithmetic is: $2,250 initial margin minus a 33¢ or $1,650 loss equals $600.) At that point the speculator will receive a margin call for $1,650 to bring his account back to the required initial margin.

These examples use Board of Trade contracts of 5,000 bushels each. Since corn, wheat, and soybean contracts on the Mid-America Commodity Exchange call for only 1,000 bushels, margin requirements are less, but are handled in a similar manner.

Hedge Margins Usually Start at Maintenance. . .

Margins work somewhat differently for hedgers than for speculators. The hedger's margin requirement generally begins at the maintenance level, kept good.

In the same situation as the speculative example above: to sell a contract of beans, the hedger will need to keep at least $1,500 in the account at all times.

For example, if he deposited only $1,500 (and of course he would start with more), he would be subject to a margin call the first day prices rose above his entry point. He would have to deposit more money or close out his short position. If the same farmer started the same hedge with $2,000, the excess money over $1,500 would be shifted out of the margin column as prices went against his position.

When prices rose more than 10¢ per bushel, the hedger would have to deposit more money or be subject to a closeout due to an under-margined account.

The point is, when you hedge in the futures markets, you should be prepared for the margin call eventually. And, so should any banker who is helping finance your hedge.

There should be enough capital backing the hedge to cover more than minor market moves against your position, and there may be times when you'll want enough to cover substantial adversity.

An example might be a weather market. You're convinced excited speculators have pushed prices well beyond levels indicated by actual crop damage.

If you're brave enough to trade it, such a market could offer you excellent profit potential through a short hedge. But, it's extremely difficult to judge the best time to initiate the short sale.

As a result, you also had better be brave enough to recognize the potential for substantial adversity against your position and set stop-loss protection accordingly.

Say, for example, you hedge a volatile market with 5¢ stop-loss protection. That stop is hit. So you hedge again at a higher price with another close 5¢ stop. You could well be knocked out of the market both times—and therefore extremely hesitant to try it again. As a result, you're out $500, plus commissions, to the futures market—and still without hedging protection.

It's good to keep reminding yourself that the object of a hedge is to "lock in" a price that offers a profit. But, that price objective may be "locked in" only if you hold the hedge into the expiring contract month when the futures and cash price should be converging.

What's lost in the cash commodity, which you own, should be made up for in part or full in the futures position which you also control.

The farmer who puts a close stop on his short hedge position is not hedging. In effect, he's speculating that the market is so bearish it can't produce a substantial rally.

And, as is often the case with speculators, he may be right about the long term market direction and still cheat himself out of the opportunity to take advantage of the move.

You Should Have Fail Safe Stop. . .

That's not to say the hedger should never pull out of a hedged position no matter what develops. The 1973 soybean market and some others since then have made that clear.

Margin requirements expanded so rapidly in the winter-spring period of 1973 that a single new-crop soybean contract, hedged at $1,500 maintenance margin in January, mushroomed to more than $14,000 margin by May. That requirement jumped much higher through summer, but there weren't many farmers left in the market by then.

So, in the original hedging plan you work out with your broker and banker, there should be a point where you refuse to stay hedged. An example might be a close above heavy resistance into new contract high ground. That, as we will explain in our discussion of chart formations, can precede a move to substantially higher levels.

So, there should be a fail safe stop on many hedges—an area where you want to get out and reevaluate your position with the idea of reinstating it later.

However, those areas are not as numerous as some brokers might have you believe. The term "selective hedging" rings sour with some farmers who have been whipsawed in and out of a hedged position.

Our point is that a lot of thought needs to go into the initial decision of at what price level to make a hedge. Just as much thought should go into the decision to close a hedge out before you're ready to sell the cash product.

The Broker

Hedging is a team effort by you and a broker. Failure most often occurs when broker or hedger, or both, fall down in their responsibility to the team.

Your primary responsibility is to have your goals and objectives for hedging clearly defined. You should have a firm knowledge of production expenses and at what levels your hedges are locking in a profit over production costs. You should have a line of credit to meet margins.

Also, the better your understanding of the commodity futures markets and how they work, the better your chance for success. More often than farmers like to believe, the reason for failure lies with the hedger.

Your broker's primary responsibility to you is accurate, up-to-date market information, and the knowledge and means *and time* for applying that information to your specific hedging goals.

Willingness to spend time on your behalf is important. The duties of the average commodity broker are many. A partial list would include:

Market Analyst—Responsible for keeping current on and projecting the impact of daily fundamentals in a wide variety of commodities in addition to those you are interested in as a farmer-hedger.

Market Technician—As adept at reading the technical, speculative pulse of the market as he is at interpreting the day-to-day impact of supply-demand fundamentals.

Trading Strategist—Able to build trading programs consistent with the different temperaments, goals, and resources of his individual speculative and hedging clients.

Order Specialist—Responsible for getting the best fills possible on all market orders whether they be speculative or hedging.

Margin Man—Normally it's your broker who notifies you when your account is undermargined. It's not his favorite duty, but he must keep his accounts in line with exchange requirements and those of his own firm.

Remember that in fulfilling these duties and others, most of the broker's time is taken up with speculative accounts. The speculator's goal is different from yours as a hedger. He will be in and out of the market much more often than you—therefore demanding more of the broker's time and contributing considerably more to his commission income.

Your best chance for success lies in finding a broker who handles hedging accounts efficiently despite this potential conflict from the speculative side of his business.

And, when you find the right man, remember that the better your understanding of the commodity futures markets and how they work, the more efficiently you can employ the limited time a busy broker has available.

The Technical Market

Anyone engaged in any form of commerce, from marketing corn to selling lemonade at a neighborhood stand, recognizes the importance of supply versus demand as a price making force.

Supply-demand fundamentals are equally important in the futures market. But, these markets have another side—often more dominant in determining short term price action.

That other side of the futures market is the "technical" side. It's not concerned with the size of the wheat crop or daily slaughter figures or growing conditions.

The technical market is concerned with people. It's a measure of what speculators and hedgers are thinking.

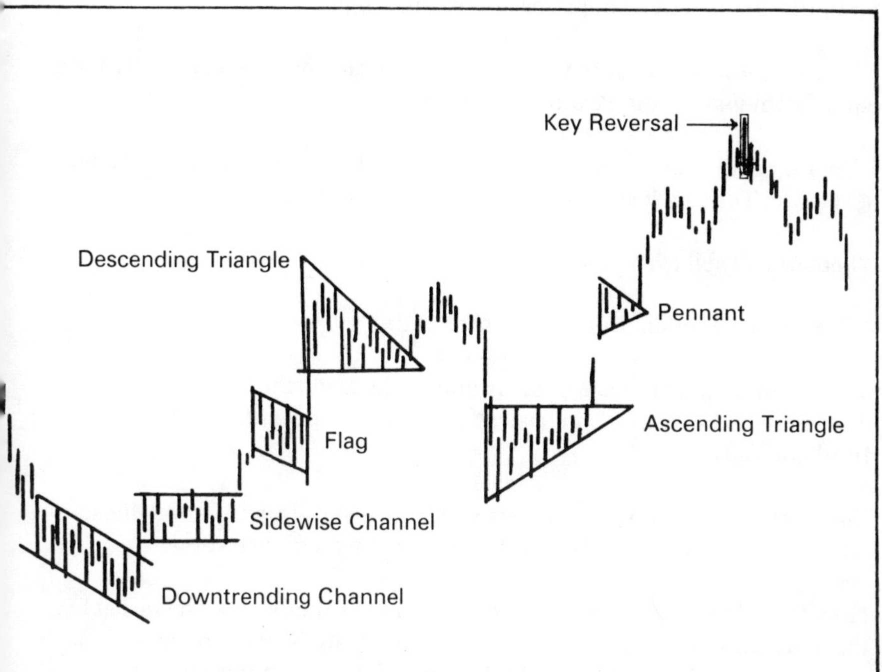

Supply-demand statistics play the dominant role in how high or low prices may go. But, people determine how prices will achieve that level.

How many times have you heard a neighbor say he missed a good market price, not because he didn't expect it, but because it just took longer to get there than he expected? As a result, he sold too early.

For every farmer saying that, there are scores of speculators bemoaning the fact they were right about a price move, but actually lost money on in and out trades while the market was achieving the anticipated level.

The truth is that in the futures markets there are thousands of people every day determining prices for ten times that many reasons.

Here are a few reactions to a government crop report—actual reactions from traders on the floor of the Board of Trade as reported on the Commodity News Service wire:

"This will provide strength for soybeans."

vs.

"I think current soybean prices are way too high."

— — — — — —

"That soybean figure sure won't push the market down—especially with significant losses being claimed in Iowa."

vs.

"This is an all-time record in soybeans. I can't in good conscience be long anymore. That big loss in Iowa is baloney."

— — — — — —

"People will sell corn as a result of this report."

vs.

"Corn is an excellent buy on any 1¢ to 2¢ dip."

— — — — — —

These comments are from professionals who trade the markets every day and who have access to basically the same supply-demand fundamentals.

But that's what makes the markets work. Unless opinions varied, those who wanted to sell wouldn't find anyone to buy and vice versa.

How then do we put a finger on the dominant attitude about a market by those who are participating in it? Price movement is one indicator. . .so are volume and open interest. Let's take a look at them individually, beginning with price patterns.

Chart Price Patterns

There are people trading in commodity futures markets who say they couldn't care less how much acreage has been planted, what yield prospects are, or how many animals are in the nation's feedlots.

These traders are chartists. The pure chartist concerns himself only with the daily, weekly, and monthly gyrations of commodity chart lines in making his buy and sell decisions.

To farmers, who traditionally think in terms of the fundamental aspects of the market, the chartist may sound like a strange breed. In the realm of commodity trading he's not. In fact, all good commodity traders incorporate some technical chart study into every trading decision they make.

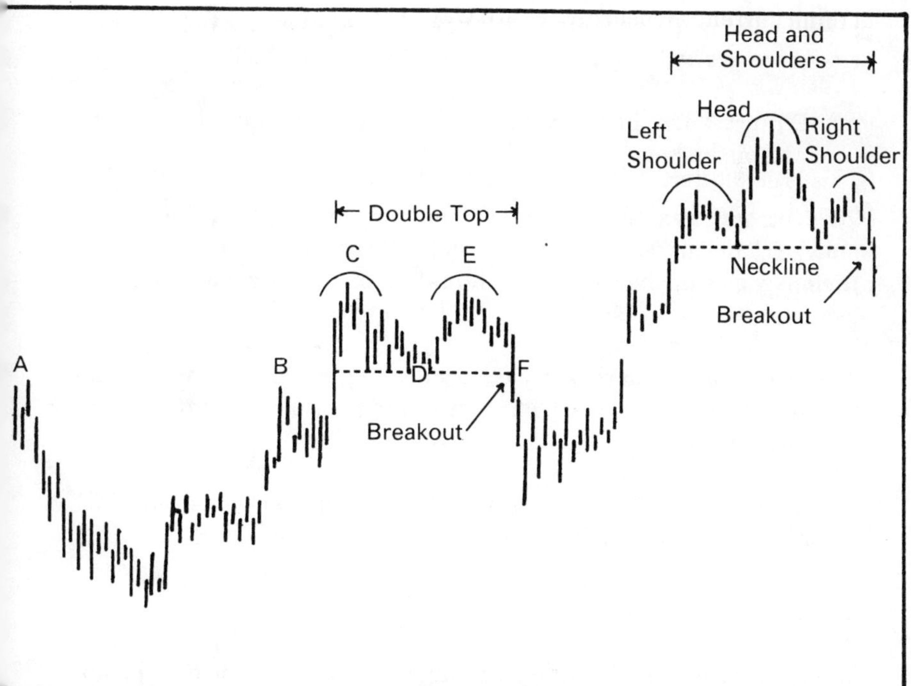

One point you should understand clearly is that chart formations do not forecast market moves. However, they can help point out where "resistance" or "support" areas have developed on the charts. As a result, they can be a guide in timing hedges or cash sales.

We're not going into all the chart formations with which some traders say they work. However, we will discuss a few of the dominant ones to help you better understand when your broker refers to them.

The Double Top

Among the more impressive formations are the "Double Top" and the "Head and Shoulders." The Double Top can signal the end of a major bull move.

To form a Double Top the market pushed into new highs (Point C on the chart)—a move that is followed in order by a price decline (D), a move back to the earlier highs (E), then downward price pressure which eventually penetrates the lows established on the previous decline (F).

Basically, Points D and E are resistance levels—resistance to further price increases by traders who believe values are too high.

Point D represents a price level where bullish traders collectively took a stand and pushed prices up again.

However, once bearish forces muster enough strength to push prices below "D," the market can drop dramatically as those who had bought previously give up their stand and liquidate, or sell back their long position.

At the same time, traders who have been sitting on the sideline awaiting a sell signal are encouraged by the break and pressure the market with additional new selling.

Reverse of a Double Top is a Double Bottom, which can signal a turn to higher levels after a sustained downmove.

The Head and Shoulders

The classic Head and Shoulders formation has signaled the final death rattle of many past bull markets.

The formation begins with a strong upmove to new life of contract price highs, followed by a market reaction which completes the left shoulder. Prices then surge again to new contract highs.

The new highs are followed by another price drop which completes the head, then an abortive rally which forms the right shoulder.

A line drawn from the low of the left shoulder through the low of the right shoulder depicts the neckline. The formation is completed when prices close below that neckline.

In a dynamic market, a major decline may already have occurred by the time the complete Head and Shoulders is formed. However, a rule of thumb among traders is that once the neckline of a Head and Shoulders formation collapses, the subsequent downmove could at least equal the distance from the top of the head to the neckline.

Opposite of a Head and Shoulders is a Reverse Head and Shoulders, which can signal the turn around from a bear market to a bull market move.

WHY FORMATIONS DEVELOP

Why does the market tend to react much the same way following the completion of one of these formations? It's not magic. The reasons have to do with people in the market and what they expect to happen after the formations develop. In part, they are a self-fulfilling prophecy.

But, the nuts and bolts of chart formations have more substance than that. Let's take a closer look.

Trendlines and Channels

Possibly one of the most intriguing phenomena of commodity futures charts is the way price patterns often tend to channel themselves. Although they can't accurately be called formations, these uptrending, downtrending, and sidewise channels are the most basic of the price patterns.

A breakthrough *below* the *uptrend line* in a rising market (Point A) or *above* the *downtrend line* in a falling market (Point B) can signal a temporary price reversal.

PRICE CHANNELS

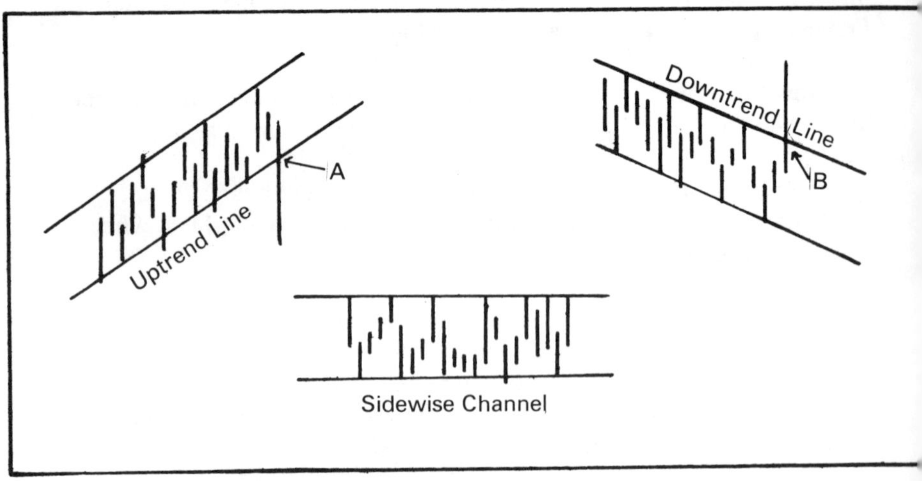

Basically, in an uptrending channel there are sufficient sellers at the top and buyers at the bottom to keep prices in the channel until something significant happens to break them out of it.

A break below the uptrend line can indicate that the bears, or sellers, have finally amassed sufficient fundamental power to break the rising market trend—or perhaps more accurately, that the fundamentals have forced some of the buyers in the channel to give up. The way they give up is to liquidate their long positions with offsetting short sales, which helps pressure the market.

Support and Resistance Chart Points

Another way to describe the top and bottom of a channel is in terms of "Support" and "Resistance" areas—two very important concepts in chart analysis and words you'll hear often from your broker.

In a sidewise channel, the top boundary represents "a resistance" (to higher prices) area and the bottom is a "support" (under the market) area.

The market tends to move into a sidewise trading pattern when there is considerable doubt about eventual price direction. It's a pattern you might see in a market evaluating crop prospects before harvest begins.

Crop size is in doubt, but those who have traveled through an Iowa drought area may have a different concept than those who have been exposed to an entirely different situation in central Illinois where weather was ideal.

A patchwork quilt of these conditions across the Corn Belt can make it extremely difficult for anyone to estimate actual production until harvest begins.

So the market moves into a sidewise pattern with upper boundaries manned by those who are more generally optimistic about the crop than those supporting, or buying, at the lower boundary.

You can see why these boundaries become important. If harvest returns begin to confirm a smaller crop than the median estimate, the price will again push to the top of the channel.

And if the harvest indeed turns sour, time comes when that resistance can't hold. Prices close out of the top of the channel.

That breakout encourages new buying by sideline traders willing to jump into the market once they believe a direction has been established.

But, equally important, the close is a red flag to "short" traders who had been selling to provide the resistance at the upper end of the channel.

Many will abandon that short position once the resistance area breaks. In fact, most of them will have placed "buy" stops above the resistance to get out of the market if prices close in new high ground. Pressure of that buying itself pushes values higher.

So you have the double impact of new buying, plus buying back by traders who had been short the market. That's not magic. It's simply a matter of spoils for the victor.

Often, the longer the market trades in a sidewise pattern, the more dramatic the price move in the direction of the breakout once the support or resistance areas are violated.

An important point to remember is that market channels are not the only support and resistance areas that develop on a price chart. *All past chart areas where prices have made a significant reversal in direction are prime targets to develop resistance or support areas at some future date.*

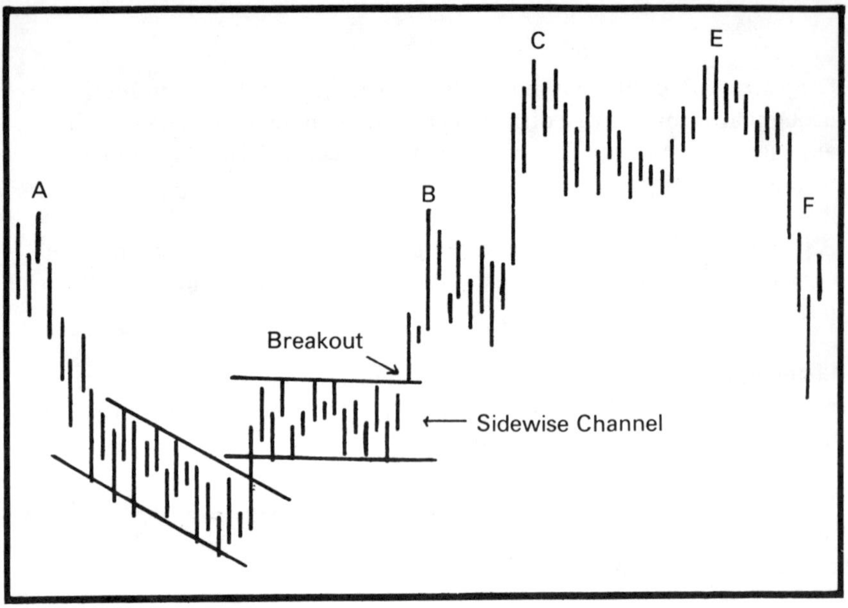

A logical resistance area once prices break through the top of the sidewise channel illustrated here is back at Point A, the previous contract high.

It's this same type of thinking that forms the second hump of a Double Top formation. The highs made in the first top (Point C) become a chart resistance area—an eventual testing ground for those who would try to push the market higher.

Knowing that, traders who are long the market may be inclined to take profits at what they consider the resistance area. And, sideline traders with a bearish bent look at the area as a calculated place to sell. So may "short" hedgers.

Triangles

The name pretty well describes this fairly common, but often important, formation. Dominant types are ascending and descending triangles.

Since it takes some time to amass a major triangle formation, considerable resistance develops at its base.

Therefore, a breakout through the upper level of an ascending triangle (A_1-C_1) or the lower end of a descending triangle (B-C) can be a fairly significant signal for a strong move in the direction of the breakout.

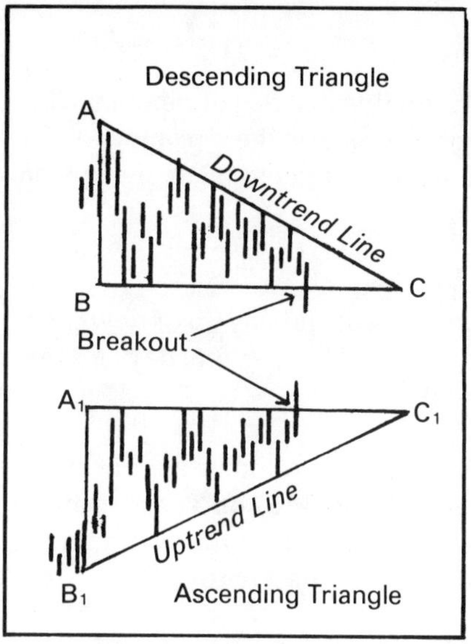

A breakout and close below the uptrend line of an ascending triangle quite often signals a move at least back to resistance at the bottom corner (Point B_1).

A close above the downtrend line of a descending triangle can signal a move back to resistance at its apex (Point A).

If that move back to "A" is made, the descending triangle will often become part of a larger formation, possibly a Double Top if market fundamentals turn bearish. Or, the triangle may become the left Shoulder of a Head and Shoulder formation if a new, higher price level is achieved.

Flags and Pennants

These formations begin with a sharp upmove in a bull market or sharp downmove in a bear market. In a bullish situation a flag or pennant may form after a breakout above a heavy resistance area with the initial upmove forming the flagstaff.

Flags and pennants represent consolidation areas—areas where the market pauses to assess whether fundamentals indicate the move has reached its course or should continue.

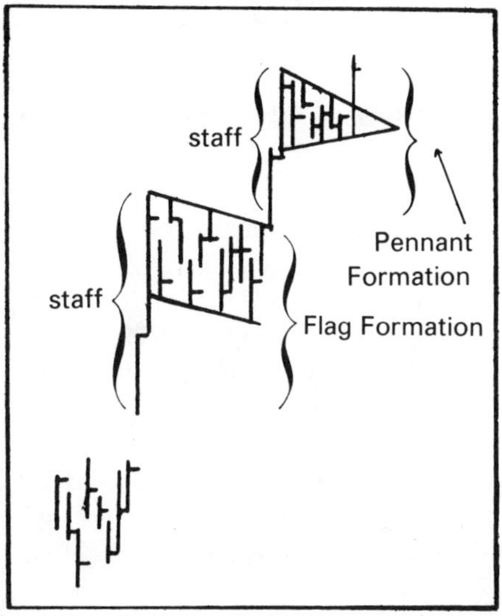

They may also represent areas where traders who helped build the flagstaff are willing to take some profits—an action which helps cause a pause in the move.

Since this type of profit taking occurs on nearly every strong market move, flags and pennants are fairly common. A general rule of thumb is that they often represent the mid-range of the eventual move.

A breakout on the upside of the downtrend line of a flag or pennant can often precipitate a move at least back to resistance at the top of the flagstaff. And a break above there signals further potential on the upside.

Gaps

Often in a highly excited market, prices move so quickly up or down that they leave gaps, areas where no trading occurs between one day and the next.

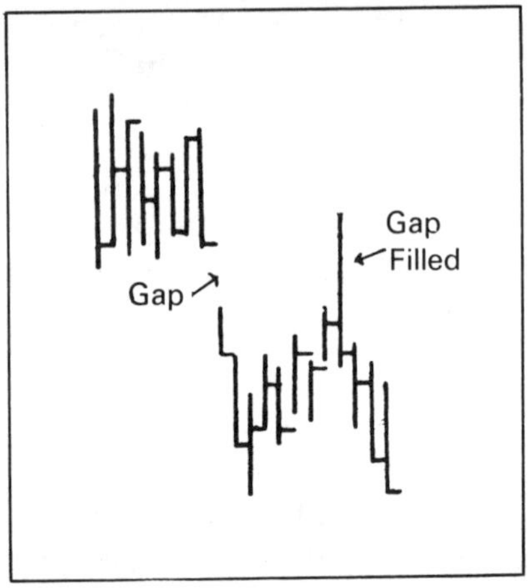

An example would be a soybean market close at $7 on Tuesday and an open at, and continued trading above, $7.20 on Wednesday.

We won't go into all the types of gaps. The important point to remember is that gaps often become targets for traders—areas to be filled in eventually, possibly days or weeks after they have formed.

It's as if the market consciously tries to tidy up the unsightly holes left by an out of control situation from the past. A trader wanting to short a chart that shows a gap somewhat above current levels may well put a market order in at the gap, figuring chances are good it will be filled before the expected price drop begins.

Key Reversals

What technical signal is available in the futures markets to tell you that a runaway price move might be over?

Nothing is reliable in this situation. However, a technical signal that the market at least is ready for a breather is a "key reversal" day.

A key reversal doesn't always signal the end of a major move. However, it often signals at least a temporary pause in the action, possibly becoming part of the stem in a flag or pennant formation.

In a bull market, ingredients of a key reversal day are: (1) a high volume day when (2) the highest price exceeds the previous day's high, and (3) the market reacts sharply (normally down limit) to close on its low. That low has to be under the previous day's low.

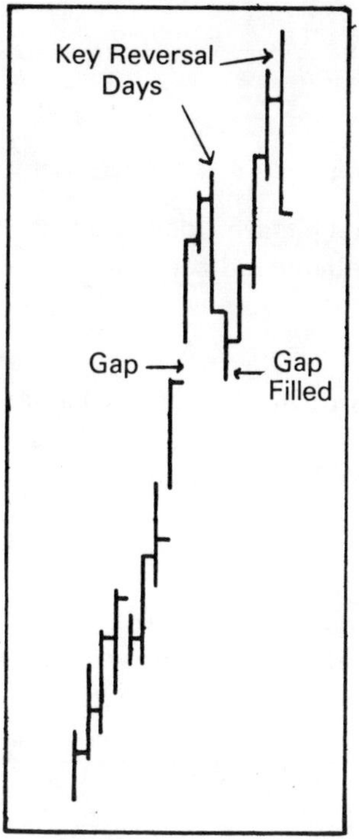

A key reversal day out of a *bear market* also exhibits high trading volume. Prices push to new lows, then recover strongly to close on the day's high and above the previous day's high.

Is it hocus-pocus? Certainly it must seem that way to farmers who traditionally think almost exclusively in terms of the fundamental or supply-demand aspects of the market.

In the end, of course, fundamental forces such as production, disappearance, weather, and government policy will dictate eventual market values.

However, if you are considering a cash sale or hedge because:

(1) You are fairly certain prices are near the potential highs indicated by fundamental supply-demand forces, and

(2) The price being offered is good enough to give you an acceptable profit . . .

. . . your main concern becomes the best point to make your move. Chart patterns can become a guide. So, at times, can volume and open interest.

Open Interest And Volume

Since they only provide a part of the total market picture, open interest and volume by themselves aren't completely reliable indicators of anything.

However, in conjunction with price, they can provide clues as to whether a futures market will continue its current course or is staging itself for a reversal. Open interest figures are quoted for each delivery month in a commodity. The total for all months is used in technical analysis.

Basically, open interest represents the number of outstanding or "unliquidated" positions in the market. Open interest increases only as "new" longs and "new" shorts enter the market together.

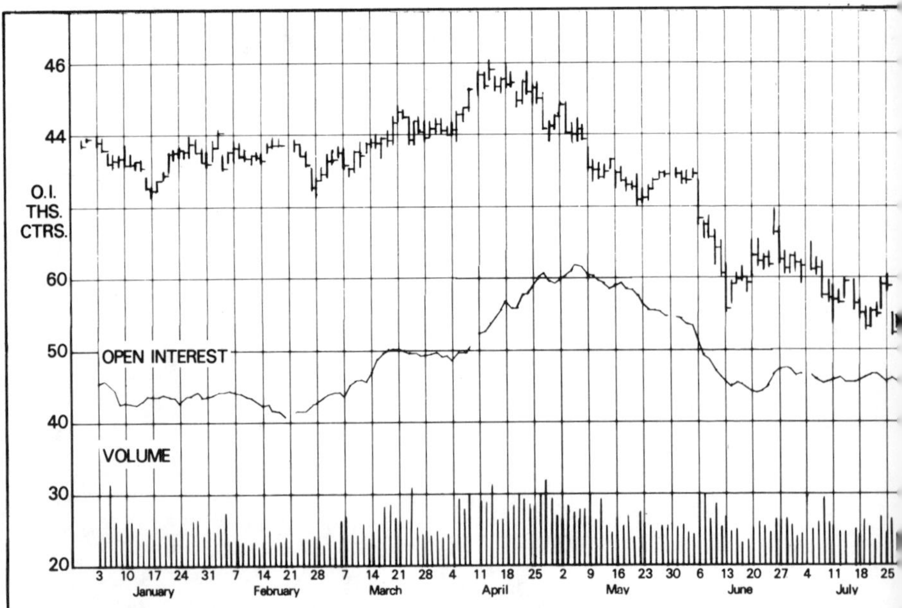

Example I: A hedger goes short 5,000 bushels of corn. His sale is taken by a speculator adding to his long position. Open interest increases by 5,000 bushels, or one contract.

Example II: A hedger goes short 5,000 bushels of corn. His sale is taken by an "old" speculator or hedger buying back a short position established a week earlier. Open interest remains unchanged.

Example III: A hedger covers (or buys in) his short position from a speculator or hedger who is liquidating a long position established a week earlier. Open interest drops by one.

Used in conjunction with price, open interest figures can help measure the technical well being of a market.

In general:

**If price and open interest are both moving up, the market is in a strong technical condition.*

The fact that both are increasing indicated that new longs are aggressively coming into the market and willing to pay successively higher prices for the privilege.

**If price is up while open interest is declining, the technical understructure of the market may be weak despite rising values.*

It probably means prices are moving up because those who have sold the market are buying back their positions from "old" longs who are willing to take profits. Buying action by "shorts" lifts prices. But since they are buying from longs already in the market, open interest drops.

**If price is down while open interest is rising, the market is in good technical shape for the decline with trader opinion generally accepting potential for lower prices.*

The falling prices and increasing open interest denote new bears aggressively selling.

**If prices are falling on declining open interest, the market may be setting itself up for a reversal to higher prices.*

The falling open interest indicated longs in the market are selling contracts back to shorts, who are ready to take profits because they believe prices are about as low as they can go in the current move.

Since there are normal seasonal ups and downs in open interest throughout the year (up during harvest, down in later months, etc.), any percentage increase over a period of time should be compared with the year-earlier period at least, and farther back if possible.

Volume Measures Momentum. . .

Daily volume is a measure of the total trades made. On any given day, volume will be much lower than open interest because the vast majority of traders in the market don't get in and out in the same day.

Therefore, open interest is an indicator of broad scale public interest or participation in the market. Volume is that too, plus an indicator of momentum.

During a technically strong price upmove, open interest and volume tend to move with prices, building as the price moves up, dropping on price reactions.

The rising open interest is indicative of new buyers willing to come into the market at higher prices, and rising volume points to continuing upside momentum.

There are traders willing to go short, but they aren't as resolute in their opinion as the longs, who in their willingness to buy keep the uptrend going.

However, a day when price declines on much heavier volume than the previous day can indicate loss of momentum on the upside. It may signal that both bears and bulls were equally resolute in their trading, but the bears eventually won the day.

An example is the topping out action described earlier in our discussion of the "Key Reversal" formation.

On that day, established bullish momentum pushes early prices into new high ground. But bearish interests persist. So do bullish interests, but after much in-fighting the tide begins to turn.

Prices falter. Bullish resolution begins to wane. Bearish resolution intensifies. Prices start to crumble, then collapse completely as longs with profits to protect give up. The market closes on its low, below the previous day's low.

High volume, declining prices: The momentum has shifted from the upside to the downside. The shift may be temporary or sustained, depending at what level bullish forces are able to regroup.

Sound like war in the trenches? It is.

Knowing Your Basis

In July, your elevator is offering $2.86 on a forward contract for new-crop corn that you know has to be sold at harvest. December futures are $3.36. That's a basis of 50¢, cash under December futures.

You foresee a good crop and expect harvest cash prices could drop, possibly to the $2.70 level. As a result, you're willing to sell part of your crop now rather than risk lower fall prices. But, which is your better offer—the forward contract or a hedge in December futures?

The answer revolves around your local basis. Knowing the basis, or the usual price range between your local cash markets and the nearby futures *during the month in which you are considering a sale,* can be extremely helpful in estimating the approximate price the futures market is offering. Also, knowing the basis will help you evaluate whether a forward cash contract being offered is in line with reality.

Let's use the opening paragraph figures for examples. In addition, we'll assume that in the past six years your local cash basis during the October harvest period has ranged from cash 17¢ under December futures at the narrowest basis level to cash 41¢ under December futures at the widest level. The average October basis was in the vicinity of 30¢ below December futures during the past six years. (See table.)

OCTOBER BASIS TABLE: YOURTOWN, ILLINOIS

CASH CORN VS DECEMBER FUTURES

WIDEST BASIS				CLOSEST BASIS			
DATE	CASH	DEC.	BASIS	DATE	CASH	DEC.	BASIS
10/23/75	$2.42	$2.83	– 41¢	10/ 2/75	$2.63	$2.97	– 34¢
10/28/76	$2.12	$2.52	– 40¢	10/ 7/76	$2.43	$2.76	– 33¢
10/ 6/77	$1.74	$2.12	– 38¢	10/27/77	$1.84	$2.10	– 26¢
10/ 5/78	$2.01	$2.29	– 28¢	10/26/78	$2.17	$2.37	– 20¢
10/25/79	$2.36	$2.66	– 30¢	10/ 4/79	$2.74	$2.91	– 17¢
10/23/80	$3.28	$3.68	– 40¢	10/ 2/80	$3.20	$3.43	– 23¢

Therefore, basis history indicates the $3.36 offered in December futures represents a potential minimum of $2.95 (the $3.36 December futures minus 41¢, the widest historical October basis).

A maximum of $3.19 per bushel appears possible ($3.36 minus 17¢, the narrowest historical October basis). On the average, December futures appear to be offering somewhere around $3.06 for the corn ($3.36 minus the average October basis of 30¢).

The last two years' figures argue strongly for an October basis below the six-year average. However, increased interest rates and storage costs may widen the basis more than the table of historical prices above would indicate.

As a result, you have a decision to make. If the basis runs back to the narrowest level by October, you'll be better off hedging in the futures market. If it widens out to the widest level of recent years, you'll be ahead to sell cash now and forget about hedging.

You're expecting a large crop and lower prices at harvest. Those are conditions that promote a wide basis as cash prices weaken under pressure of excess corn looking for a home.

As a result, you wouldn't be surprised by an October basis in the vicinity of 40¢, cash under December futures.

The elevator obviously concurs with your analysis of harvest price pressure since he is offering 50¢ under December futures—historically wide by 9¢.

It's a situation where the hedge looks more attractive than the cash offer. Here's how it works.

DATE	CASH CORN		DEC. FUTURES		BASIS
July 21	Passed up offer of	$2.86	Sold at	$3.36	–50¢
October 6	Sold cash corn at	$2.70	Bought at	$3.12	–42¢
	Price change	– $ .16		– $ .24	

On July 1, you passed up a cash offer of $2.86. Instead you hedged in December futures at $3.36. On October 6, you sold your cash corn for $2.70 per bushel, 16¢ under the July 21 cash offer. But at the same time you closed out your December futures hedge—buying it back at $3.12 for a 24¢ profit.

In short, the hedge made you an extra 8¢ per bushel profit over the summer cash offer ($2.70 + $ .24 = $2.94).

What if the July 21 cash contract offer had been $3.06, or 30¢ under December futures? If you use the same rationale as above, the cash offer looks better than the hedge.

If you went the hedging route and basis widened to the 42¢ level, the hedge would net you less than accepting the cash offer.

DATE	CASH OFFER	DECEMBER FUTURES	BASIS
July 21	$3.06	$3.36	–30¢
October 16	$2.70	$3.12	–42¢
	–$ .36	–$ .24	

By hedging, you get $2.70 for cash corn plus 24¢ on the hedge, or $2.94 per bushel minus hedging costs, versus the $3.06 forward cash offer.

The point is that a knowledge of basis is important in evaluating cash offers. It can also help determine whether a hedge is feasible.

The Storage Hedge: An Important, But Neglected, Farm Marketing Tool

Narrowed down to the basics, farmers have three possible selling periods. . .before, during, or after harvest. Also, they have two basic avenues to make those sales. They can either sell for cash or in some way get involved with the commodity futures markets.

BASIC MARKETING ALTERNATIVES

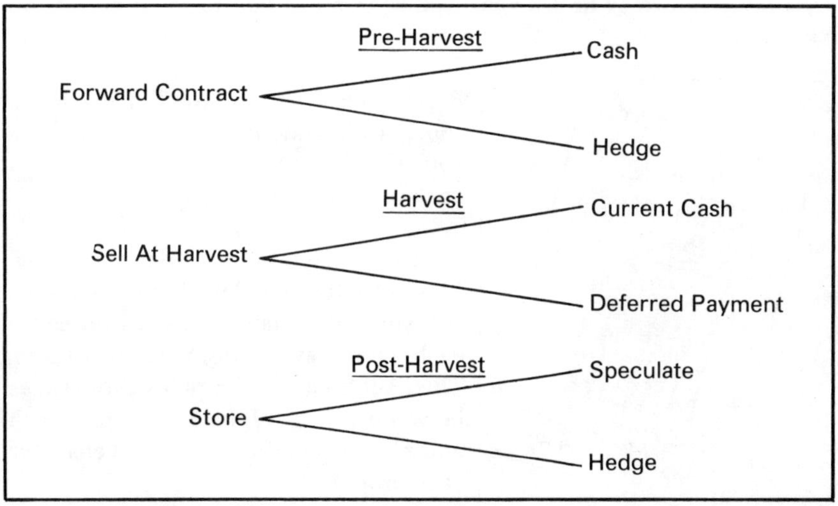

The vast majority of farmers feel most comfortable with the cash alternatives—either forward cash contracting, selling out of the field, or storing and speculating that the cash market will rise enough to cover storage costs plus some additional profit.

The majority of farmers feel very uncomfortable with the futures market alternative. It's too bad this problem exists, because as the diagram indicated, the farmer loses one half of his marketing alternatives when he ignores the futures markets. That's like milking only one side of the cow.

The key to intelligent hedging is to KNOW YOUR BASIS. You've heard that so many times it probably sounds trite. But it's so fundamental to hedging we're not ashamed to repeat it.

HOW TO DETERMINE YOUR BASIS

How do you get to know your basis—or the normal difference between your local cash offer and Chicago futures in any given period? Well, you have to do some work.

An important first step is to begin keeping a daily record of your local cash markets relative to Chicago futures. A method we've suggested is to take a small notebook and paste in each day's futures prices, clipped from the local paper. Then pencil in your local elevator offer for the same day.

By simply referring to last year, you're in a position to see how current bids compare.

But for best results, you'll need to do some additional homework. We think you should track basis relationships back at least 3 years.

It doesn't have to be a daily tracking. You can select one day of the week—i.e., plot your local cash and futures price for each Thursday during past crop years. Then subtract the Thursday differences between Chicago futures and local cash and plot those differences on a chart for each crop year.

Based on St. Louis cash corn, the charts on the following page show how the local cash/July futures basis looks for the 1977-78 through 1979-80 crop years. Note how the price spread between cash and futures narrows in quickly once harvest is past. That narrowing of the basis is what makes the storage hedge work.

WHAT HAPPENS WHEN YOU HEDGE?

In a storage hedge, you keep (store) the cash product and sell an equal amount in the futures market.

In effect, you are:

Long (have bought or maintained title to) the cash product, and

Short (have sold) the futures market.

Object: To lock in an acceptable profit and to pick up storage or basis gains as the futures contract matures.

Examples of Storage Hedges. . .

On October 16, 1975:

- Chicago cash corn was $2.75 per bushel.
- Chicago July futures were $3.08 per bushel.

In other words the harvest market showed a 33¢ basis ($3.08 – $2.75), Chicago cash under the July.

Farmer Darrow, who farms just west of Chicago, felt the $3.08 being offered by July futures was a worthwhile return. (He remembered a few years not long before when much less looked entirely adequate.)

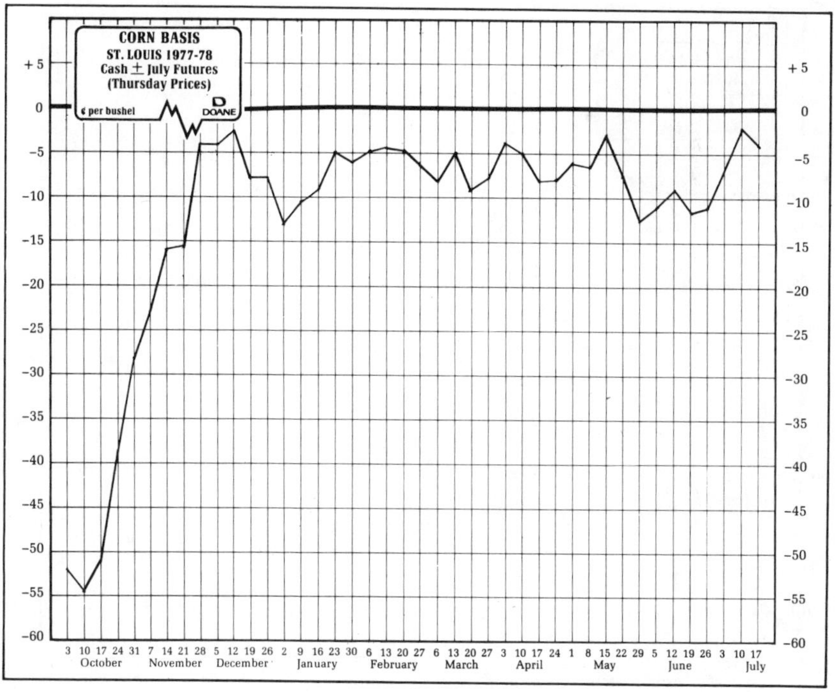

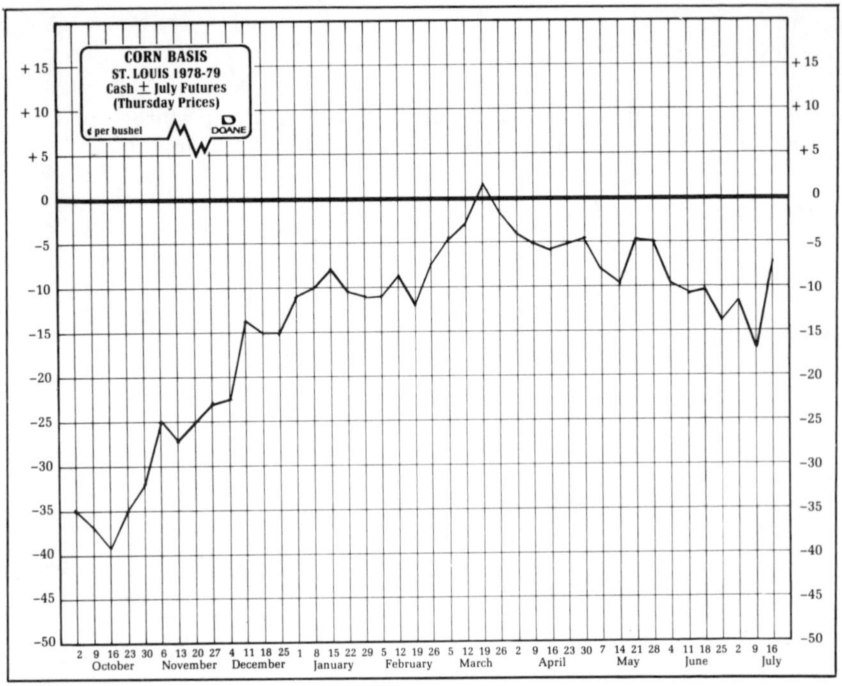
CORN BASIS
ST. LOUIS 1978-79
Cash ± July Futures
(Thursday Prices)
¢ per bushel
DOANE
October
November
December
January
February
March
April
May
June
July

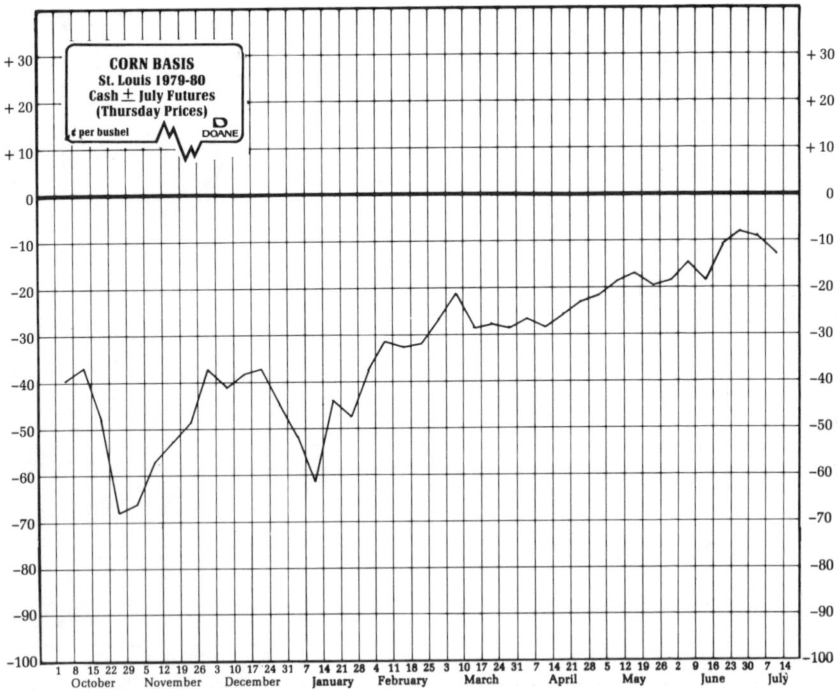
CORN BASIS
St. Louis 1979-80
Cash ± July Futures
(Thursday Prices)
¢ per bushel
DOANE
October
November
December
January
February
March
April
May
June
July

He also knew that the 33¢ basis (or difference between Chicago cash and the July futures) was abnormally wide based on years before 1975. And he knew no matter how wide the harvest basis, cash and futures prices tend to run together as futures contracts expire. In fact, in his area the July 1 cash price had actually run above July futures over the past five years—by about 2¢ on average.

In effect then, based on historical basis relationships for his area, July futures were potentially offering him somewhere in the vicinity of 35¢ per bushel to store his corn until July.

So he hedged 5,000 bushels that had just gone into storage. He did it by selling one contract of July corn on October 16. On the following July 1, he sold the cash corn and bought in the July futures contract.

THE TRANSACTION WAS:

CASH CORN		JULY FUTURES	
October 16 (stored worth)	$2.75	(Sold at)	$3.08
July 1 (sold at)	$2.93	(Bought at)	$2.96
Change from October 16	+$ .18	Change from October 16	–$ .12

In total then, he received $3.05 per bushel for his corn on July 1. . .$2.93 cash plus 12¢ per bushel made on the short July futures transaction. The $3.05 was close to his original goal of $3.08.

The market paid 30¢ per bushel to store his corn into July. Because of that storage payment, he received $3.05 per bushel for his effort versus $2.93 had he sold July 1 without a hedge and $2.75 had he sold from the field. In short, hedging allows you to lock in an acceptable profit long before you actually release your grain.

If cash prices fall, your profit goal is protected by the futures which should also be under pressure as the futures contract expires.

Hedge Insulates Against Profit Windfall, Too . . .

As you are aware from reading many hedging examples, if prices rise during a storage hedge, your profits will be insulated also. You won't make as much if you're hedged during a price upswing as you would unhedged.

Here are the kinds of markets Farmer Darrow was looking at in 1973:

On October 11, 1973:

- Chicago cash corn was $2.54 per bushel.
- Chicago July futures were $2.74 per bushel.

Farmer Darrow had felt $2.74 the futures offered was a fair return (highest for that date in some years). And the 20¢ basis between the cash and July futures also was better that average relative to previous mid-Octobers.

So he hedged 5,000 bushels. He did it on October 11 by selling one contract of July futures to cover cash corn that had just been put into storage.

THE TRANSACTION WAS:

CASH CORN		JULY FUTURES	
October 11 (stored worth)	$2.54	(Sold at)	$2.74
July 1 (sold at)	$3.12	(Bought at)	$3.07
Change from October 11	+$ .58	Change from October 11	+$ .33

In total, he received $2.79 per bushel for his corn ($3.12 cash minus 33¢ per bushel lost on the short hedge). Remember, if you're short the futures and they go up, you lose.

Actually the $2.79 was 5¢ better than his original goal and 25¢ above the October 11 cash sales. But it was 33¢ below the $3.12 per bushel an unhedged July 3 would have brought.

Of course, if he had been firmly convinced cash corn was going much higher after the hedge was placed, he could have lifted it quite easily by buying in his July futures contract—a procedure that is not nearly as simple for corn sold on a forward cash basis.

In short, the futures market allowed Farmer Darrow the flexibility to quickly become a cash speculator again any time he wished, simply by lifting his hedge.

How Basis Charts Help

The St. Louis basis charts on pages 45 and 46 again illustrate that basis characteristically narrows from harvest into the expiration of any upcoming futures contract. They also show that:

(1) The extent the basis narrows will vary each year, depending on fundamentals working in the market.

(2) Although cash and futures tend to move toward each other as futures contracts grow older, the process is anything but smooth. Reactions, sometimes severe ones, occur throughout the life of the contract.

(3) Most of the basis narrowing out of the harvesttime glut occurs by January. This is a vital characteristic of basis in these days of burdensome interest rates, which argue against holding grain any longer than you must.

Here's a closer look at these basis characteristics with the help of basis charts we've compiled.

The charts on the next two pages show the 1978-79 July soybean basis for Laurel, Iowa, and Memphis, Tennessee. That basis is plotted against the strongest and weakest levels that cash beans sold under the Chicago July futures over the previous three years. The three-year average basis (1975-76 through 1977-78 crop years) runs through those two extremes (the solid line).

By using this type of chart, the farmer can compare current year basis action with: (a) the previous three-year average and (b) the widest and narrowest basis levels that made up that three-year average. This information is important in making hedging decisions.

A daily tracking is best, but not necessary. Here we use every other Thursday prices. Here's how you use the charts.

Let's say we're interested in soybean basis information for early January in Laurel, Iowa. The chart shows that for that period in the crop years

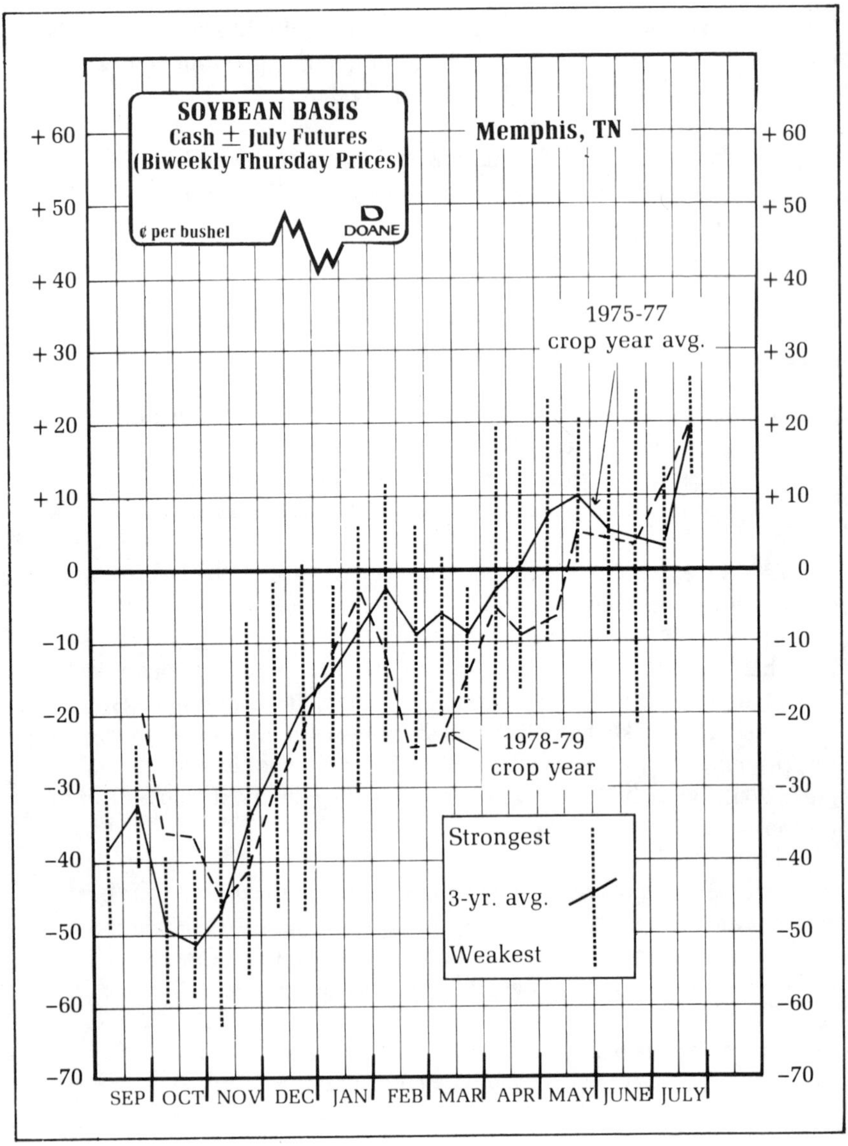
SOYBEAN BASIS
Cash ± July Futures
(Biweekly Thursday Prices)
¢ per bushel
DOANE
Memphis, TN
1975-77
crop year avg.
1978-79
crop year
Strongest
3-yr. avg.
Weakest
+60
+50
+40
+30
+20
+10
0
−10
−20
−30
−40
−50
−60
−70
SEP
OCT
NOV
DEC
JAN
FEB
MAR
APR
MAY
JUNE
JULY

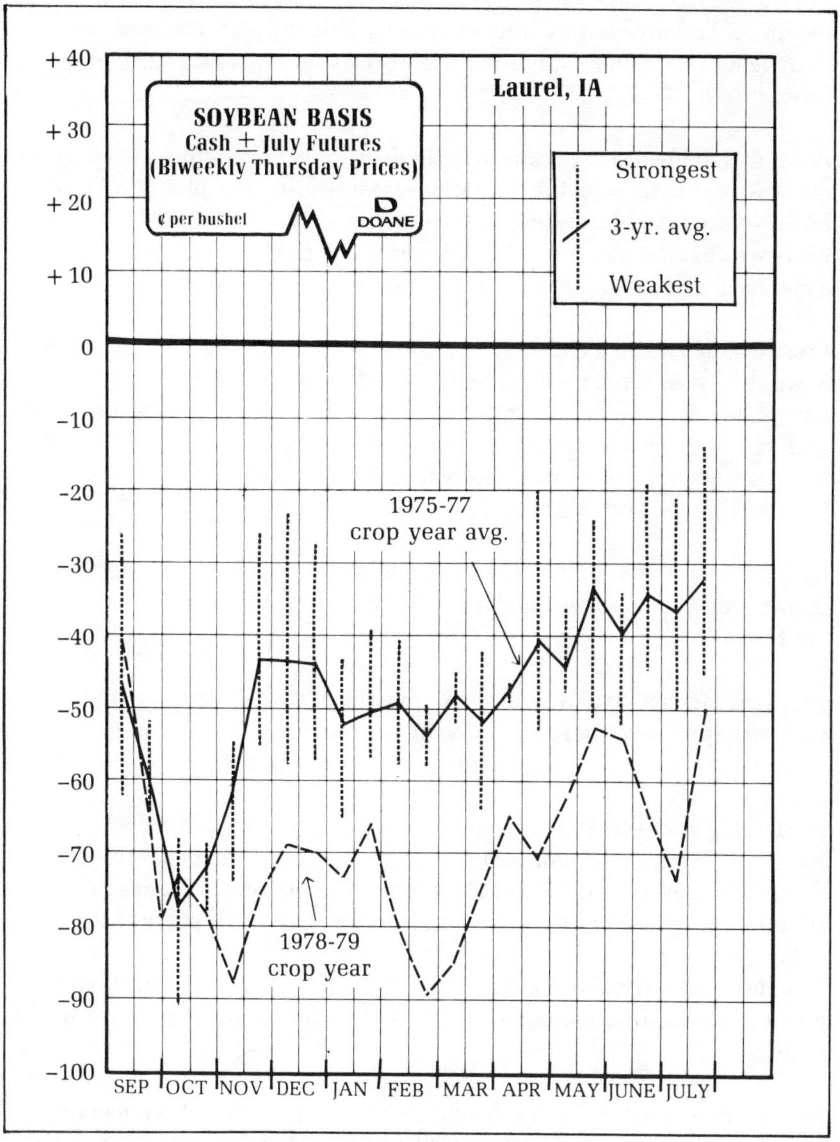
Laurel, IA
SOYBEAN BASIS
Cash ± July Futures
(Biweekly Thursday Prices)
¢ per bushel
DOANE
Strongest
3-yr. avg.
Weakest
+40
+30
+20
+10
0
-10
-20
-30
-40
-50
-60
-70
-80
-90
-100
1975-77
crop year avg.
1978-79
crop year
SEP
OCT
NOV
DEC
JAN
FEB
MAR
APR
MAY
JUNE
JULY

1975-76, 1976-77, and 1977-78 the bid for cash soybeans at Laurel has averaged 52¢ under July futures (or -52¢ basis the July).

For those three years, the chart also tells us the weakest level Laurel cash beans sold relative to July futures in early January was -65¢, and the strongest early January basis in those three years was -42¢, cash under July futures.

Against that historical perspective the Laurel farmer wanting to compare current year basis with the immediate past would have plotted 1978-79 basis—the dashed line. And, as the year progressed he would see that his basis was historically wide through almost all the life of the July futures contract and in early January was some 74¢ under the July.

Contrast the Laurel basis situation with Memphis. As you'd expect, the Memphis basis is narrower (or stronger) than an interior point like Laurel, Iowa. As you move into the interior, basis levels characteristically widen. For example, in early October 1979 the cash versus 1980 March futures soybean basis was -36¢, cash under, at Toledo, Ohio; -54¢ in Central Illinois; and -$1.06 in Laurel.

Basis tells you how badly local buyers want your product. A stronger than normal basis generally denotes a stronger than normal demand in your area.

The demand can be temporary, and may be localized. That's why basis will vary from past years and why, at any one time period, it may be improving more in your area than in some other areas.

In offering a weaker than normal cash basis, users are saying supply is adequate. They'll take your crop, but first they will deduct the full cost of storage from now until the time they can use it or move it. More than adequate supplies are what contribute to the wide basis at harvesttime.

A wider than normal basis also can occur when speculative enthusiasm pushes futures up at a much faster pace than fundamentals allow for cash.

For example, during the 1979 soybean harvest the basis at Woolstock, Iowa, moved to $1.42 under July 1980 futures. That compared to a three-year average of -66¢ for mid-October.

Part of the basis was a low cash price suffering from transportation difficulties and burdensome harvest supplies. However, at the same time, speculators were keeping the Chicago futures market strong, partly in response to record bull moves in gold and silver. The combination of weak cash and strong futures pushed the basis to record levels.

Basis Guides Hedging Decisions

As we just noted, cash offers sometimes get way out of line with historical reality. One way to compensate for an extremely wide basis is to hedge.

To make that decision you need to know your historical basis, the current basis, and what basis is likely to be when you're ready to lift your hedge. It's all available to you if you keep basis data similar to that shown on basis charts. They tell you how much basis improvement to expect, a help if you want to hedge at harvest.

Sometimes basis widens at periods other than harvest. For example, in late February 1979, the price difference between Laurel, Iowa cash soybeans and July 1979 futures fell to -89¢. That's opposed to a three-year average for the period of -53¢, cash under July futures (see chart on page 51.)

The -89¢ extreme was due in part to speculative demand for futures, demand created by trader response to Brazil's drought.

(We're using Laurel basis as an example here. But, a similar pattern probably showed in your local cash to July futures basis relationship, particularly if you're in interior Iowa.)

What kind of hedging opportunity was the Laurel basis offering at -89¢ under the July?

Well, our three-year average chart shows the bulk of the cash to July futures basis move in Laurel was made by late May. The average basis in late May for the three years was -34¢, cash under the July. The weakest late-May basis was -51¢. Put in table form, here's how the numbers would look.

1979 Laurel Basis in Late February			Historical Laurel Basis in Late May		
July Futures	**Laurel Cash**	**Basis**	**Strongest**	**Average**	**Weakest**
$7.89	$7.00	−89¢	−22¢	−34¢	−51¢

Based on the three-year average of the normal and the weakest late-May basis then, the February basis of -89¢ appeared to be offering Laurel farmers 38¢ to 55¢ more per bushel to hedge (minus hedging costs) than to sell outright for cash.

That would more than make up for the cost of storing the crop for an additional three months, even in commercial storage. If the late-May basis pushed back to -22¢, the difference would be about 67¢ more received per bushel.

That's what history said could result from a late February hedge. What actually happened? We'll use actual 1979 prices in the table below to find out.

Laurel, Iowa Soybeans

Date	Cash	July Futures	Basis
Feb. 22, 1979	$7.00	$7.89	-89¢
May 24, 1979	6.82	7.35	-53¢
Change	–.18¢	–.54¢	+ 36¢ (Basis improvement)

As the table shows, the actual May 24 basis fell outside the three-year historical average. It was 2¢ lower than the widest historical basis—a characteristic of Laurel and many other interior points for the entire year.

Note the late-July basis was -50¢, under, nearly 7¢ wider than the previous three-year low.

A reason basis levels are widening is the increased cost of storage and, particularly, high interest rates.

In any event, the actual hedge brought the Laurel farmer $7.36 per bushel before hedging costs ($6.82 cash + 54¢ made in the short July futures positions).

Holding and selling cash on May 24 would have brought him $6.82 per bushel minus storage costs.

What would he have made by selling cash on February 22 and earning 8% interest on the money? That interest would have made him about 14¢ per bushel over the three-month period according to our tables. Grain in commercial storage would cost an additional 6¢ for the three-month period.

So actual value of the hedged beans on May 24 was $7.36 - 14¢ (interest opportunity lost) minus 6¢ (commercial storage) minus 1¢ (futures commission). That comes to $7.15 per bushel.

Actual value if he had on-farm storage was closer to $7.21 versus the $7 offer in late February.

However, we want to emphasize again that the cost of storage and therefore hedging is going up. Interest rates of 14% or better are available through certificates of deposit or money market instruments.

Part of these expenses will be worked into the basis, and you probably can look for wider than average levels in the years ahead.

But hedging opportunities will remain, as illustrated by the record $1.42 cash/July harvest basis we noted earlier in Woolstock, Iowa.

Delayed Pricing: Not for the Inexperienced

On July 2, 1975, cash corn in north central Illinois was selling at a 21¢ premium to September futures. Normally, north central Illinois cash is at a 10¢ to 20¢ discount to September futures in early July.

The table shows how the transaction worked that summer if a north central Illinois farmer DP'd corn on July 2, and asked for payment August 14:

Date	Cash	Sept. Futures	Basis
July 2, 1975	$2.73	$2.53	+ 20¢
August 14, 1975	3.07	3.21	−14¢
Change	+ .34	+ .68	−34¢

The farmer received $3.07 per bushel on August 14, some 34¢ better than the July 2 price. The elevator received $2.73 (for its July 2 cash sale) plus 68¢ on its long September futures position, also for a profit of 34¢ per bushel, not including margin and interest earnings.

No wonder DP caught on under those conditions. Both the farmer and the elevator made out like bandits. Delayed pricing received considerable attention by word of mouth and in the farm press. Farmers wanted to see more of it. Elevators tried to accommodate them — even during harvest.

Problem is, since a delayed pricing transaction is basically the reverse of a storage hedging transaction, it figures the best time for a storage hedge (harvest) is not the optimum time (and, in fact, may be the worst time) for deferred pricing.

In fact, delayed pricing is not a game for amateurs, and even the most sophisticated elevator managers have been burned by it at times. To come out on a DP contract, the elevator has to predict with some degree of accuracy how basis relationships will change from the time the farmer delivers the grain until he asks for payment. If the elevator service fee is 15¢ per bushel and the basis moves in 35¢, the elevator has lost 20¢ per bushel on the transaction.

Here's an example: A farmer short on storage takes an elevator offer to DP corn. The farmer is charged a 15¢ per bushel service fee.

When the grain is delivered, the elevator manager moves it on to a processor, receiving a margin of 8¢ per bushel over his board price for that day. The elevator then buys March futures, which it will hold until the farmer says to sell. It's been agreed the farmer must sell before March 1. The table shows the transaction.

Date	Cash	March Futures	Basis
October 15	$2.70	$3.20	−50¢
February 22	2.90	3.05	−15¢
Change	+.20	−.15	+35¢

The farmer asked for payment on February 22 with cash corn at $2.90 — 20¢ over the cash price when the DP agreement was established in October. That's a 5¢ per bushel gain for the farmer, but it's 20¢ more than the elevator would have had to pay in October.

In addition, the elevator lost 15¢ per bushel on the long March futures position. In effect, the elevator received $2.99 per bushel for the corn ($2.70 + 15¢ service fee + 8¢ margin + 6¢ interest on the $2.70 per bushel cash banked from October to February).

BASIS: CASH ± FUTURES

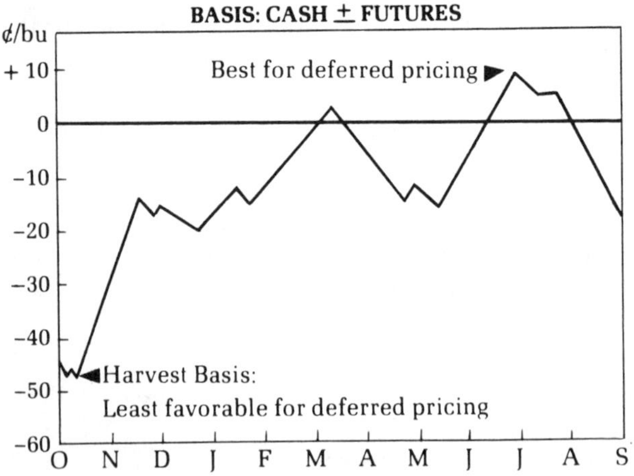

But, the elevator eventually paid $3.05 for the completed transaction, i.e., $2.90 paid to the farmer and 15¢ paid to the futures market, excluding commissions.

The reason the elevator lost is because it misjudged the impact of basis improvement from October to February. The basis closed 35¢ per bushel. The elevator only charged a 15¢ service fee. To protect its 8¢ margin, the elevator should have charged at least a 29¢ fee (35¢ - 6¢ interest earnings).

If the elevator's losses are great enough to force bankruptcy, the farmer loses too. That's because the farmer transfers ownership of the grain to the elevator when he moves into a DP arrangement. If the elevator goes under, the farmer is left as an unsecured creditor.

In light of these considerations, you should never use DP, right? Not necessarily, but harvest would appear to be the least opportune time to use it, for both the farmer and the elevator. By late spring or early summer, the basis often has been narrow enough that the elevator can offer DP at no service charge. The risk is much less because the basis usually is at its narrowest point during spring or summer.

"Basis Contract" Less Risky

A less risky form of pricing from the elevator's standpoint is a "basis contract" in which payment to the farmer is tied to a specific futures contract. For example, the elevator might receive the cash grain at harvest and promise to pay the farmer 50¢ under the March futures on any day of the farmer's choosing before March 1.

Let's take the same prices used in the DP example and see how a "basis contract" set at 50¢ off the March would work out for the farmer and for the elevator when the elevator is working with an 8¢ profit margin.

Date	Cash	March Futures	Basis
October 15	$2.70	$3.20	−50¢
February 22	2.90	3.05	−15¢
Change	+.20	−.15	+35¢

The farmer asks for payment on February 22 when March corn futures are trading at $3.05. Therefore, he receives $2.55 per bushel for corn ($3.05 March futures minus the 50¢ basis that existed when he delivered the grain during harvest).

The elevator receives $2.63 for the corn ($2.70 + 8¢ margin minus 15¢ lost on the long March futures position). In effect, he bought the corn for $2.55 and sold it for $2.63. His 8¢ margin had been protected.

Had the market moved to $3.20 cash and $3.35 March futures for the February 22 sale, the farmer would have received $1.75 per bushel, some 15¢ better than the harvesttime sale. The elevator's earnings would have remained at the 8¢ margin originally planned. Here's how:

Date	Cash	March Futures	Basis
October 15	$2.70	$3.20	−50¢
February 22	3.20	3.35	−15¢
Change	+.50	+.15	+35¢

The elevator pays the farmer $2.85 per bushel. He receives $2.93 ($2.70 plus 8¢ margin plus 15¢ made on the long March futures).

In short, the elevator was using the basis contract to protect an 8¢ per bushel margin. The farmer was using it to speculate that post harvest price recovery would exceed the improvement in the basis.

Even so, it's at this point the farmer may feel he has come out on the short end of the transaction. If he didn't fully understand the procedure when he entered into the basis contract, he would undoubtedly resent receiving $2.55 cash payment in the first example and $2.85 in the second example, when actual cash prices were $2.90 and $3.20.

But, as we noted earlier, nothing comes free, neither building sufficient on-farm storage to handle the harvest glut, nor being forced to sell at the harvesttime basis. Storage costs don't disappear through some magic manipulation of the futures market.

Using Livestock Futures

Livestock futures markets offer producers the same management options as do futures markets for crops. Actively traded futures markets exist for fed cattle, feeder cattle, and hogs. Used correctly, they can help minimize a hedger's price risks by shifting them to another party.

The futures market is not a panacea. The fact that it is available for hedging doesn't automatically ease management decisions. In fact, in some ways futures markets can make decisions more difficult by opening another alternative in the marketing program. Carefully analyze all choices before making your decision. Hedging isn't advisable for everyone and every situation.

Hedging is a mechanism for setting the effective selling price in advance. It is important for the prospective hedger to realize hedging protects against price declines but also shuts off the possibility of reaping the benefits of price rises, so long as the hedge is in place.

So, why hedge? For the most part, hedgers do so because they consider the offered price attractive in terms of allowing or assuring an attractive profit margin and/or a price higher than expected cash prices at the forward time in question.

Good Information: A Key

There are at least three "must" pieces of information if one is to make a rational hedging decision. First, you must know your cost of production. Otherwise, there is no way of evaluating a forward or futures price in terms of profit potential. Second, you need to have an opinion of likely market trends—an opinion of likely prices when the livestock is ready for market. Third, one must know his normal "basis" near contract expiration time. Without this knowledge, one cannot estimate what price level a given hedge will actually "lock in."

Basis baffles many would-be users of the futures market. The word is trade jargon for the difference between the futures price and the cash price. The basis for any given point or local market will usually vary within a relatively narrow band when contracts approach expiration.

It is this predictability of basis that makes hedging workable. If you can predict your basis accurately, you can hedge with reasonable precision.

The price you lock in via a hedge will be: *(Price of futures contract) – (basis) – (trading costs)*. For example, December live cattle (fed cattle) are trading at $70, and your normal basis against that contract is $2. Trading cost, including broker's commission and interest on margin deposit, is estimated at 50¢.

In this case, by hedging you can effectively lock in a local price of $67.50 ($70 – 2 – .50). You may want to lock it in for some or all of the cattle you plan to produce in that time period if $67.50 looks like a profitable price or if you think cash prices in December will likely be lower than $67.50.

Finished Product Versus Contract Specifications

Futures contracts and quotes relate to a specific quality and quantity of animals. (See page 73 for specifications.) The live cattle futures specifies Choice steers, for example. Can off-spec livestock be hedged? Yes, if you can with acceptable accuracy anticipate the price difference between your product and that specified in the contract.

Suppose you have heifers instead of steers. If heifers are usually, say, $2 below steers, you would make a further adjustment in the futures price. Applied to the figures above, you could hedge in a price of about $65.50 on heifers.

One important difference would be that the heifers would not be deliverable to satisfy the contract. In this case, you would have to get out of the contract by an offsetting purchase. As a practical matter, hedges are usually lifted via an offsetting purchase. However, one has the option to make delivery on the contract if his product meets the specifications.

Livestock Hedging Examples

The following example assumes that the hedger will complete his hedge by taking an offsetting futures position, rather than delivering. Also, the hedger's estimates of his basis prove accurate.

Suppose in early August a feeder expects to put a new group of steers on feed. He believes they will be ready to market in December, so he makes the following calculations to evaluate a possible hedge.

Laid in Cost	
112 head x 730 lbs x 63.92¢ =	$ 52,260.99
Feeding Costs	
112 head x 345 lbs x 70.09¢ =	27,082.78
Total Cost	79,343.77
Cost per pound = $\frac{\$79{,}343.77}{(112 \times 1{,}075)}$ =	65.90¢/lb

The table below demonstrates how to estimate potential hedging return on the live beef hedge once you've determined production cost.

December live beef futures		$69.68/cwt
Less localizing costs		
a. Transportation (variable, depending on producer's location)	.20	
b. Shrink (calculated for producer's location)	.30	
c. Marketing cost at delivery point	.25	
d. Quality adjustment (obtained from estimating type of livestock producer will sell and adjusting from par)	.88	
e. Delivery discount (no discount in this case—delivery being made at Omaha)	.00	
f. Brokerage fee	.15	
g. Interest on margin deposit (estimated by length of time, degree of price change, and interest rate)	.20	−1.98
Expected selling price		$67.70/cwt
Less: production costs		$65.90/cwt
Potential return		$ 1.80/cwt

Forecasted cash December price: $66-68/cwt
Expected *unhedged* return: 0-$2/cwt

In the following hedging example, the finisher estimated hedging return before ever purchasing calves. Here's how he locked in the estimated $1.80 per cwt feeding profit.

In August He

Sold:	**Bought:**
3 December live cattle futures contracts* at $69.68/cwt	112 730-lb feeder calves at $63.92/cwt

In December He

Bought:	**Sold:**
3 December live cattle futures contracts at $67.23/cwt	112 1,075-lb finished steers at $65.40/cwt

This is how the total transaction breaks down. After subtracting feed and other costs on the cash transaction, the feeder had:

Costs	$ 79,343.77
Cash return	78,741.60
Loss on cash transaction	$ 602.17

Since the futures market also declined, the finisher made $2,760 on his hedge after commission ($180) for a net profit of $2,158. This approximates to the $1.80 per cwt he originally targeted.

*This feeder decided to hedge all of his cattle. Since one live cattle contract on the Chicago Mercantile Exchange totals 40,000 pounds, the three contracts closely approximate the total 120,400 pounds of live animal weight the producer expects to market. A farmer may, however, decide to hedge only part of his livestock. A typical partial hedge might cover one-third to two-thirds of the animals he will actually market.

The Buying Hedge: An Option for Feeders

Many livestock producers also have the option of using a long (buying) hedge to lock in some of their production costs. A producer may do this months before he needs items such as replacement cattle or feed ingredients. The buying hedge simply assures him that later he will pay no more for these items than the price he hedges them for today.

In a buying hedge, the feeder must still localize the futures price. However, he *buys* a futures contract that will mature about the time he needs the production item (feeder cattle, grains). This position is then offset when he sells back the contract and buys feeders or grain in the cash market.

Lock-In Cost of Replacement Animals

In July, a cattle feeder evaluated November feeder cattle futures by subtracting his expected basis from the futures quote.

November futures	$66.20/cwt
Less localizing cost (basis)	2.00
Estimated November cash purchase price	$64.20/cwt

He expects that he'll have to pay more than the estimated $64.20 per cwt for feeders next fall, so he locks in this price by hedging. Here's how he does it:

In July He

Buys:	Sells:
2 November feeder cattle futures contracts (42,000 lbs each) at $66.20/cwt	(no offsetting cash transaction at this point)

In November He

Sells:	Buys:
2 November feeder cattle contracts at $69.64/cwt	120 700-lb feeders at $67.50/cwt

Cash and futures prices both went up before November. The finisher had to pay $67.50 per cwt for feeder steers laid in the lot in November. Here are the results of the cattleman's hedge. Compare them to the unhedged feeders purchase.

The gain on the futures transaction was $2,769.60 after commission ($120). But the cattleman had to pay more than the price he targeted in July for the feeders ($2,772). Thus, the two transactions offset each other, giving him very nearly the price he targeted.

Predetermine Feed Costs

Assume that the feeder expects to see feed costs rise but doesn't want to, or can't, take immediate delivery on grain. A combination of grain and livestock hedges can lock in acceptable feed costs *and* slaughter cattle sale profits.

A good way to manage both risks would be to go long grain and short live cattle futures. The grain hedge will also pin down feed costs to help the cattleman set up his short live cattle hedge.

Unlike the short grain storage hedge, once the feedgrain futures are bought, the buying (long) hedge is often not held in place until contract delivery month. Rather, the grain futures are sold back as actual grain purchases become necessary.

The feeder has, in effect, prepriced a portion of his production costs. His cost for grain is approximately the price targeted earlier.

A hog operator could also set up this combination livestock-feed hedge. He would follow the steps outlined above using prices and costs for his own area and operation.

Margin Requirements

Requirements for margin deposits should be well understood by a livestock producer before he places a hedge. Margin is money the hedger must deposit when the trade is initiated. If the market goes against your hedge, you may be subject to a margin call requesting additional capital.

Remember that you went into your hedged position satisfied with a specific potential profit based on the likelihood that the cash and futures prices would approach the basis you normally see at your market when a futures contract expires. What you may lose in the cash transaction you should pick up in part or in total in the futures trade.

However, you may have to go through some adversity in your futures account even though you're right in the final analysis. It may require additional margin capital. You should be prepared for this when you place your hedge, and so should your banker if he's helping to finance it.

Multiple Hedging

Some economists feel that multiple hedging strategies offer livestock producers more profit than a "hedge and hold" strategy. Following the multiple hedge strategy, a hedge might be lifted and replaced many times between its first placement and the actual delivery month. For this reason, its critics argue that multiple hedging verges on speculation.

Timing the movement of your hedge depends on when you feel you need the protection of a hedge versus those times when you feel that the market is stable or on the upswing. A decision on when to lift, hold, or enter a hedge may be based on one of a number of technical systems.

One such system relies on signals provided by moving weighted averages of daily closing prices. When the market breaks out above or below the weighted average of these factors for a certain number of days, it's time to lift or replace your hedge, depending on the direction of the breakout.

Most multiple hedging strategies employ a systematic approach, as opposed to sheer speculation. But, it is still easy to succumb to the pressure of daily price fluctuations and make a bad—and in futures markets, this means expensive—decision. At best, multiple hedging is probably not for the beginner.

Chicago Board of Trade
Soybean Complex Futures

	Soybeans	Soybean Meal	Soybean Oil
Basic Trading Unit	5,000 bushels	100 tons	60,000 pounds
Deliverable Grade	No. 2 Yellow and substitutions at differentials established by the Exchange	One grade of meal only, with minimum protein of 44%—see Exchange Regulations for exact specifications	One grade of crude soybean oil only—see Exchange Regulations for exact specifications
Delivery Points and Differentials	Chicago at par and Toledo at an 8¢ per bushel discount	Shipping plants in six territories, with par at Decatur, IL; and other locations at differentials determined according to Exchange regulations	Warehouses in the Midwest with Decatur, IL, at par; and other locations at differentials that are freight adjusted to Decatur, IL—New York City
Delivery Instrument	Registered warehouse receipts issued by warehouses approved by the Exchange	Shipping certificates--from shipping plants approved by the Exchange	Registered warehouse receipts issued by warehouses approved by the Exchange
Price Quotation	Cents and quarter cents per bushel	Dollars and cents per ton	Dollars and cents per hundredweight
Minimum Fluctuation	¼¢ per bushel or $12.50 per contract	10¢ per ton or $10 per contract	1/100th¢ per pound or $6 per contract
Daily Price Limit	30¢ per bushel ($1,500 per contract) above and below the previous day's settlement prices	$10 per ton ($1,000 per contract) above and below the previous day's settlement price	1¢ per pound ($600 per contract) above and below the previous day's settlement price
***Initial Margin**	$2,250 per contract	$1,350 per contract	$900 per contract
***Hedging Margin (Maintenance)**	$1,500 per contract	$900 per contract	$600 per contract
Hours of Trading (Mon.-Fri. Central Time)	9:30 am to 1:15 pm	9:30 am to 1:15 pm	9:30 am to 1:15 pm

*Margins are subject to change. Margins required by member firms may exceed contract margins.

Chicago Board of Trade

	Corn Futures	Wheat Futures
Basic Trading Unit	5,000 bushels	5,000 bushels
Deliverable Grade	No. 2 Yellow and substitutions at differentials established by the Exchange	No. 2 Soft Red, No. 2 Hard Red Winter, No. 2 Dark Northern Spring, No. 1 Northern Spring, and substitutions at differentials established by the Exchange
Delivery Points and Differentials	Chicago at par and Toledo and St. Louis at a 4¢ per bushel discount	Chicago at par and Toledo at a 2¢ per bushel discount
Delivery Instrument	Registered warehouse receipts issued by warehouses approved by the Exchange	Registered warehouse receipts issued by warehouses approved by the Exchange
Price Quotation	Cents and quarter cents per bushel	Cents and quarter cents per bushel
Minimum Fluctuation	1/4¢ per bushel ($12.50 per contract)	1/4¢ per bushel ($12.50 per contract)
Daily Price Limit	10¢ per bushel (500 per contract) above and below the previous day's settlement price	20¢ per bushel ($1,000 per contract) above and below the previous day's settlement price
***Initial Margin**	$600 per contract	$1,250 per contract
***Hedging Margin**	$500 per contract	$1,000 per contract
Trading Hours (Mon.-Fri. Central Time)	9:30 am to 1:15 pm	9:30 am to 1:15 pm

*Margins are subject to change. Margins required by member firms may exceed contract margins.

Chicago Mercantile Exchange

	Slaughter Cattle	Feeder Cattle	Live Hog
Basic Trading Unit	40,000 pounds	42,000 pounds[2]	30,000 pounds
Delivery Mos.	Jan., Feb., Apr., June, Aug., Oct., Dec.	Jan., Mar., Apr., May, Aug., Sept., Oct., Nov.	Feb., Apr., June, July, Aug., Oct., Dec.
Delivery Sites	**Par delivery:** Peoria and Joliet, IL; Omaha, NE; Sioux City, IA; Guymon, OK; and Greely, CO[1]	**Par delivery:** Omaha, NE; Sioux City, IA **Others:** St. Paul, MN; Greeley, CO; Kansas City, MO; St. Joseph, MO; Dodge City, KS; Wichita, KS; Oklahoma City, OK[3]; Amarillo, TX	**Par delivery:** Peoria, IL **Others:** Omaha, NE; East St. Louis, IL; Sioux City, IA; St. Paul, MN; Kansas City, MO-KS; and St. Joseph, MO
Price Fluctuations			
Minimum (Value/Contract)	2½/100¢/lb ($10)	2½/100¢/lb ($10.50)	2½/100¢/lb ($7.50)
Daily Maximum (Value/Contract)	1½¢/lb ($600)	1½¢/lb ($630)	1½¢/lb ($450)
Minimum Margin			
Initial In Delivery Mo. (All Other Mos.)	$1,500 (1,200)	$1,500 (1,500)	$1,200 (900)
Hedging In Delivery Mo. (All Other Mos.)	$1,200 (900)	$1,200 (1,200)	$900 (600)
Last Trading Day	20th of delivery month	20th of delivery month	20th of delivery month
Trading Hours (Mon.-Fri.) (Central Time)	9:05 am to 12:45 pm	9:05 am to 12:45 pm	9:15 am to 12:55 pm

[1]Effective with Aug., Oct., and Dec. 1981 contracts.

[2]Is being raised to 44,000 lbs, pending CFTC sanction.

[3]Currently not a par delivery point, is being elevated to par, pending CFTC sanction.

Glossary of Terms Used in This Booklet

Basis — As used here, "basis": (1) denotes the price difference between a local cash quote and the futures, or (2) designates a specific futures contract or location, i.e., "The chart breakout price is $7.80 basis Chicago cash beans."

Basis Chart — Graphic representation of cash price relative to the futures. In the charts on pages 46 and 47, "0" represents cash and futures at the same price; the "minus" figures represent the number of cents per bushel cash corn is selling under July futures, and the "plus" figures represent the cash above July futures.

Basis "Narrowing" or "Strengthening" — Situation where cash prices are gaining on nearby futures. A strong basis is one where cash values at a specified point are above the futures or only under them by a narrower than average degree. Usually indicates strong cash demand at the basis point.

Basis "Widening" or "Weakening" — Situation where cash prices are losing on nearby futures. A weak basis is one where cash values at the basis point are under the futures by a wider than normal degree. Can indicate weak demand for physical product.

Bearish — Word used to describe forces likely to put the market down.

Bullish — Pertaining to fundamental or technical forces likely to put the market up.

Carrying Charge Market — A market in which nearby to distant futures contracts are trading at successively higher prices and above the current cash offer.

Full Carrying Charge — When distant futurescontracts exceed nearby contracts by the level calculated to cover all storage costs.

Commission — Fee a brokerage firm charges a customer for filling a speculative or hedging transaction in the futures market. Ball-park figure for round-turn commission charge for corn or beans would be $60 per 5,000-bushel contract traded.

Crop Year — A crop year represents the 12-month period between the beginning of harvest of one crop and the beginning of harvest for the succeeding crop.

Crop Year Table

Wheat	June 1 through May 31
Oats	June 1 through May 31
Cotton	August 1 through July 31
Soybeans	September 1 through August 31
Corn	October 1 through September 30

Expiration of a Contract — The final trading day in a futures contract; in grains, around the third week of the delivery month. Grain contracts exist about 18 months.

Fundamental Side of the Market — Fundamentals have to do with the physical supply/demand side of the market. Important fundamentals include size of production, weather, consumption levels, and yields.

Hedging — Making an equal and opposite transaction between the cash and futures market to protect or "lock in" a specified price for some future date.

Inverted Market — A market in which the nearby futures contract and the current cash offer are trading above distant contracts. Usually indicates strong current demand for the cash product.

Go Long the Market — To buy a futures contract. Those who have bought the market are collectively called "longs."

Long Liquidation — Longs leave the market by selling out an existing position. Price drops after a bearish fundamental or technical development will often be credited to "long" liquidation.

Margin Deposit — Earnest money deposited with a brokerage firm when a position is taken in the market. Margins generally run about 10% of contract value and must be maintained at a specified minimum level while the trade or hedge exists.

Margin Call — A call for additional margin when funds in a futures or hedging account fall below levels required by your brokerage firm. Margin minimums are set by the exchanges. However, a brokerage firm can set them above that minimum.

Market Position — Your place in the market, i.e., "Short July beans at $7.80," or "Long March corn at $3.10."

"Old Crop" and "New Crop" — Old crop represents the most recent crop harvested. New crop represents the crop to be harvested for the coming crop year.

Example: On January 1, 1980, old crop corn is corn harvested during the previous fall. On that date, the old crop futures would be the expired December 1979 and March, May, July, and September 1980 contracts.

On January 1, 1980, new crop is corn to be planted in the spring and represented by the December 1979 and March, May, July, and September 1981 futures contracts.

Open Interest — The number of outstanding positions in a market at any given time.

Price Rally — A market move to higher prices.

Price Reaction — A market move to lower prices.

"Roll Over" a Hedge — Moving a hedge position from a nearby futures contract to a more distant one, either because the current contract is about to expire or the more distant future offers better profit potential.

Go Short the Market — To sell a futures contract. Those who have sold the market are collectively called "Shorts."

Short Covering — Shorts leave the market by buying back previously sold positions. Price rises after fundamental or technical developments adverse to a sold position are often credited to "Short Covering."

Stop Order — A standing market order to put a speculator or hedger out of an existing market position if a predetermined price level is touched. A stop may be activated either because a profit goal has been achieved or because price movement beyond the "stop" level would indicate the need to step aside and reevaluate the existing market position. We term the latter example a "Fail Safe Stop."

Spread Trade — Stripped to its simplest form, a speculative spread trade is the purchase (or sale) of one commodity futures contract in conjunction with the corresponding sale (or purchase) of another, i.e., "Long July/Short December Corn." The object is to profit from an anticipated move in one contract relative to another.

Spread Trade: Old Crop vs. New Crop — A speculative trade to take advantage of an anticipated change in the price relationship between the old crop year and new crop year futures contracts in a commodity.

For example: In April, a corn trader who:

(1) expects a tight old-crop supply situation based on larger than expected domestic and foreign demand, and

(2) anticipates large expansion in corn acreage for the coming crop year,

can put on a Long Old Crop (say July) versus Short New Crop (say December) Spread in anticipation that the July contract will gain on the December.

Enough traders putting on such a spread in unison can have measurable price impact, possibly forcing old-crop prices higher and pushing new-crop values lower.

Technical Side of the Market — The "people" or psychological aspect of the market. The technical market is that side which helps measure trader reaction to fundamentals. Technical tools include price formation volume and open interest. In a sense, technical traders use past chart reactions as a guide to trading current markets.

Volume — Total trades made in a market over a given period, usually expressed in daily terms.